SURPRISE WITNESS

WHAT REALLY HAPPENED *DURING* THE FLOOD

Step by Step…

Book 2 of a trilogy

TEACH Services, Inc.
www.TEACHServices.com

World rights reserved. This book or any portion thereof may not be copied or reproduced in any form or manner whatever, except as provided by law, without the written permission of the publisher, except by a reviewer who may quote brief passages in a review.

The author assumes full responsibility for the accuracy of all facts and quotations as cited in this book. The opinions expressed in this book are the author's personal views and interpretation of the Bible and do not necessarily reflect those of TEACH Services, Inc.

Copyright © 2005 Jonathan Gray, all rights reserved
Copyright © 2008 TEACH Services, Inc.
ISBN-13: 978-1-57258-554-6
Library of Congress Control Number: 2008926065

Published by
TEACH Services, Inc.
www.TEACHServices.com

About the author

Jonathan Gray has travelled the world to gather data on ancient mysteries. A serious student of pre-history, he has investigated numerous archaeological sites, and has also penetrated some largely un-explored areas, including parts of the Amazon headwaters.

Other books by Jonathan Gray

Dead Men's Secrets
Sting of the Scorpion
The Ark Conspiracy
Curse of the Hatana Gods
64 Secrets Ahead of Us
Bizarre Origin of Egypt's Ancient Gods
The Lost World of Giants
Discoveries: Questions Answered
Sinai's Exciting Secrets
Ark of the Covenant
The Killing of Paradise Planet
The Corpse Came Back
The Discovery That's Toppling Evolution
UFO Aliens: The Deadly Secret
Jesus Christ – Fact or Fake?
The Da Vinci Fraud

CONTENTS

Prologue...7

1 The event itself (a)
   THE DAY IT ENDED................................9

2 The event itself (b)
   EXPLOSION FROM HELL........................17

3 The event itself (c)
   WAVES AS FAST AS JET PLANES............30

4 The event itself (d)
   STAMPEDE..39

5 Fissures of bones (a)
   UNNATURAL GRAVEYARDS....................47

6 Fissures of bones (b)
   THE SUDDENNESS................................55

7 Frozen graveyards
   INTERRUPTED DINNER..........................67

8 Sea-life cemeteries
   THE SECRET OF LOMPOC QUARRY..........82

9 Coal
   SURPRISE FOR ADMIRAL BYRD..............91

10 Successive forests – and oil
   ONE FLOOD OR MANY?........................104

11 Human relics (a)
   LADY BLUE'S LAST VOYAGE..................109

12 Human relics (b)
   FOOTPRINTS IN COAL..........................122

13 Human relics (c)
    MEN IN EMBARRASSING PLACES............**128**

14 Those fossil gaps
    THE CASE OF THE MISSING BODIES........150

15 Living fossils
    SORRY NO CHANGE............................. 161

16 Rocks "older" at the bottom?
    DON'T TRY TO MOVE OLD BEDS............ 170

17 How rock strata formed
    WHAT MY TEACHER DIDN'T KNOW........183

18 Dinosaurs and humans
    DINOSAUR ALIVE!.................................193

    Epilogue..210

    Notes..212

    Index..229

PROLOGUE

It had been a beautiful planet.
Now all was silent... in ruins.
Earth's total population lay dead from pole to pole. Billions of bodies.

It is probably needless to say that if such a devastating event DID occur in our past, then all our conceptions of the history of this earth will have to be revised.

The fact is, there are racial legends worldwide, concerning such an event, in which the stark terror of men and women still lives on... their desperate banging on a door to get inside one survival vessel... the screams as they stampede to higher ground... a single, small group of survivors, who repopulate the planet. This is the most widespread and deeply rooted tradition on earth.

These global traditions make it crystal-clear that this Great Deluge was no mere Mesopotamian flood.

As many a scientific researcher has found, legends tend to be based on a core of fact. Many an archaeological find has been made from the clues found in such legends.

Could our present scientific establishment be wrong? Could there really have been such a worldwide disaster as the Great Flood?

In Book 1, **The Killing of Paradise Planet**, we explored that first lost world – lush, temperature-controlled, idyllic.

We hinted at the event that wiped it out.

We placed under scientific scrutiny the legendary survival vessel, Noah's Ark. The verdict was, to many, rather surprising.

Now we shall probe the tantalising mystery of THE EVENT ITSELF. What really happened that **Black November**, and in the year that followed?

Come with me now, as we drop in on him, a lone businessman, clinging to a tree...

1

The event itself (a) -
THE DAY IT ENDED

About an hour to go.
It will be all over then. If he can hold on that long.
Alone, he has climbed to a high place as the fierce waves dash higher.
The screams of the others have gone. They were swept away only minutes ago.
Now it is just the howling of the hurricane, the roar of water miles deep, over the mountains and valleys. The noise is ear-splitting, like the scream of demons on an errand of destruction.
It's so final now.
So final.

* * * * * * *

This was totally unexpected, you know. Abe was about to clinch a business deal. Suddenly the giant office building began to rock. It got worse. It was awful. He and his partner had fled into the street. The pavement was rolling up and down like waves. There were lots of people. Screaming. Running. Falling.
It kept up all afternoon. He had struggled to a higher spot. A news broadcast told of fissures opening up all over the world. They were hundreds of miles long. Now magma was shooting up through the fissures. It was happening worldwide.
Then all radio communication ceased. The sun should still have been shining. But it was dark as night. There was red fire in the sky everywhere.
Two weeks now with little sleep. It was a stampede. People. Animals. Everything, trying to escape. The sea was sweeping inland. The sky was collapsing in torrents. The forests were ablaze.
Screams. Nothing but screams. It's been so terrifying. So hopeless. So exhausting. There's no way out.

It didn't have to be.

"I could have been in that survival boat!" he shrieks. "But everyone told me that group was crazy."

Here comes a big one. Oh, it's towering so high – hundreds of feet high. It's like a skyscraper... Oh, no, God... please...

* * * * * * *

Yes, the whole event had been sudden. In Book 1 of this series we discovered some ancient **legends** hinting that the earth had been suddenly tipped on its axis.

We shall now attempt a reconstruction of the event, taking into account known **scientific evidence**.

AXIS TILTED

A sudden displacement of the earth's axis would cause the destruction of the entire surface of the planet.

This sudden change in position would leave the earth wobbling like a disturbed top – and the earth is indeed WOBBLING on its axis today.

The late George F. Dodwell, South Australian government astronomer, and director of the Adelaide Observatory, made an interesting discovery in relation to the earth's wobble.

Over 26 years, he studied what astronomers call "the secular variation of the obliquity of the ecliptic". He did an investigation of summer solstice studies at ancient sites, such as Stonehenge, Amen Ra, Eodoxus, and so on. Put simply, he studied measurements of the sun's shadow-length by ancient astronomers from five continents. Available records of the position of the sun at observed solstices showed that an exponential curve of recovery had taken place in relation to the earth's axis.

In late 1960, he wrote to Dr. Arthur J. Brandenberger, professor of photogrammetry at Ohio State University. Dodwell stated:

"I have been making during the last 26 years an extensive investigation of what we know in astronomy as the secular variation of the obliquity of the ecliptic, and from a study of the available ancient observations of the position of the sun at the solstices during the last three thousand years, I find a curve which, after allowing for all known changes, [shows] a typical exponential curve of recovery of the earth's axis after a sudden change from a former nearly vertical position to an inclination of 26½ degrees, from which it was returned to an equilibrium at the present inclination of 23½ degrees during the interval of the succeeding 3,194 years to A.D. 1850."

That is to say, the earth's axis had once been almost upright, but it had suddenly changed to a 26½ degrees tilt, from which it had been wobbling back to its present mean tilt of 23½ degrees.

Dodwell's research was confirmed by Dr. Rhodes W. Fairbridge of Columbia University, in *Science* Magazine, May 15, 1970.

Dodwell concluded that something "struck' the earth at that time. He realised that this would result in massive, worldwide flooding and catastrophic geological effects. The date of this event, from his curve of observations, is 2345 B.C. It may be a surprise to learn that this coincides precisely with the traditional date for the Great Flood, as calculated from biblical sources.

It occurred suddenly

The tilting of the planet's axis occurred suddenly, bringing terrific stresses upon the earth's surface, enough to shatter and dislocate it beyond description. The whole globe shuddered.

Cuvier, commenting that the climate changed so suddenly that Siberian mammoths were snap frozen alive, and were preserved from subsequent decay, wrote that "all hypotheses of a **gradual** cooling of the earth, or a **slow** variation of the inclination or position of the terrestrial axis, are inadequate."[1]

Caused by an OUTSIDE force

No phenomenon on earth is adequate to displace the earth's axis; it could be caused only by an **outside** force. Changes on the surface of the globe, such as the raising or lowering of a whole continent, could hardly shift the earth's poles more than 2 or 3 degrees off their axis. The smallness of the effect is negligible.

In *Geological Magazine*, a mathematician draws attention to "the vastness of the earth's size, or the enormous quantity of her motion". Then he points out: "When a mass of matter is in rotation about an axis, it cannot be made to rotate about a new one except by external force. Internal changes cannot alter the axis, only the distribution of the matter and motion about it. If the mass began to revolve about a new axis, every particle would begin to move in a different direction. What is to cause this?... Where is the force that could deflect every portion of it, and every particle of the earth into a new direction of motion?"[2]

Astronomers likewise have shown that internal terrestrial causes could not effectively alter the direction of the earth's axis. Only an **external** agent could have been responsible. As Harold Jeffreys says: "If we consider the axis of the earth's angular momentum, this can change in direction **only through couples acting on the earth from outside**."[3]

Velikovsky well might ask: "What could have played the role of couples, or a vice, acting from outside?"[4]

This much is clear:
1. The cause that triggered this event must have been **more powerful than** the agents invoked.
2. Again, the cause must have acted with great **suddenness**.

Whatever the catalyst, it was of TITANIC POWER. Some have thought that the catalyst was a planet brought close to the earth; that the close fly-by of this planet set up a gravitational pull upon the earth, disrupting its outer crust. Velikovsky suggested Venus came close. Another writer suggests it was Mars.

Halley (the discoverer of Halley's Comet) believed that it was a close-flying comet that pulled upon the earth's surface, disrupting the planet's axis and orbit.

Our moon shows impact craters. If these were the result of exposure to millions of years of minor impacts, then they should be fairly evenly distributed. But this is not so. These impact craters are NOT evenly distributed.

They are mostly on one side – the side facing earth. Venus also has craters – and, like our moon, these are NOT evenly distributed. And Mars has water craters bigger than the earth's Grand Canyon – but, it appears, not enough water to produce them.

These phenomena on the above named planets and our moon suggest catastrophe.

To explain this evidence, the following scenario has been suggested.

An ice meteor with a temperature of minus 300 degrees came through the solar system. Due to planetary attraction, its speed increased and it began to break up. (If you throw a snowball too fast, it will break apart in mid-air.)

As the ice comet flew past individual planets, some of its ice fragments would be trapped by the gravitational pull of those planets and sucked into their orbits to become rings. At least four planets have ice rings around them. One thing that puzzles astronomers is, where did this material come from?

In addition, enormous fragments of ice struck and cratered some of the planets, such as Mars. Floods would hit Mars, but then the water would vaporise and be lost into space.

As the ice comet approached earth, the gravitational stress upon it multiplied, causing it to shatter.

(It is known that as two bodies come closer to each other, the gravitational pull between them multiplies exponentially. For example, if our moon came three times closer to the earth than it is at present, the gravitational pull would not be three times greater, but nine times greater.)

As the comet approached earth, the increase in gravitational pull caused it to shatter in space. And the super cold ice "snowed" on the earth – mostly around the poles. And most of these fragments were sucked in around the north and south poles, due to the strong magnetic field of the earth.

Hitting a spinning object like the earth, this suddenly dumped load would throw the earth off axis and cause the earth to wobble.

Dr Kent Hovind theorises that the sudden dumping of ice on the poles also caused the earth's crust to crack, unleashing the "fountains of the great deep". This caused the collapse of the pre-Flood canopy, and the earth to become completely covered by water.

We can be sure of this. Some force acted upon the earth from outside. It had to be from the outside.

According to Wal Thornhill, we should expect violent electric discharges between a fly-past body and the earth. He says:

"Electric discharges between closely approaching bodies would take the form of distinctively shaped helical plasmoids....

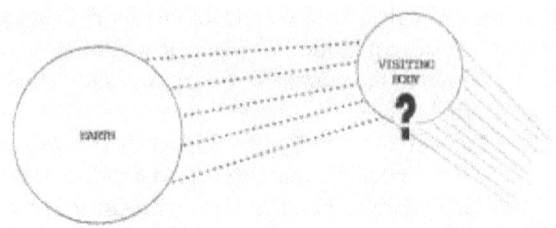

Was the outside catalyst a fly-by comet?

"When it comes to dating planetary surfaces, plasmoids cause characteristic electrical arc scarring in the form of sinuous channels and neatly circular craters with steep walls and occasional central peaks. Such craters are universally misinterpreted as impact craters. The sinuous channels are wrongly classified as riverbeds or lava channels. Minutes or hours of electrical scarring can produce a surface like that of the Moon, which is later interpreted in ad hoc fashion to be billions of years old. Hemispheric differences in cratering are expected in this model. And for the sceptics, subdued electric arc machining of a planet-sized body continues to this day on Jupiter's innermost moon, Io." [5]

Not accidental, but pre-known

But that this outside catalyst was no sudden accident we can deduce from the fact that the survivors knew several decades before the event (the book of Genesis says, 120 years).

They had time to construct an ocean liner sized survival vessel, fit and provision it, as well as take in specimens of every animal type.

And before the Great Disaster occurred, they were securely locked inside the ship – waiting.

Common sense demands that if it were an unpredicted, freak natural disaster, all this preparation could not have been TIMED so precisely. One is tempted to conclude that neither the EVENT, nor the TIMING of it was accidental. In fact, one may well ask whether the event was willed – so that external forces already under the Creator's control were set in motion?

The tilting remembered
This tilting of the earth's axis is handed down with terror-struck impressiveness in the traditions of many nations. A few examples will suffice.

- **Eskimos:** The earth tilted violently before the Flood began.
- **Mexico:** "The earth shook to its foundations. The sky sank lower towards the north. The sun, moon and stars changed their motions. The earth fell to pieces, and the waters in its bosom uprushed with violence and overflowed.... The system of the universe was totally disordered. Man had rebelled against the high gods. The sun went into eclipse, the planets altered their courses."[6]
- **China:** The earth tilted violently before the Deluge. The sky suddenly began to fall northward. The heavenly bodies changed their courses after the earth had been shaken.
- **Egypt:** The earth turned over.[7]
- **Greenland** (natives): When the Great Flood came, the earth capsized like a boat.
- The **Polynesians** and **Hindus** also related this phenomenon.

In *Tractate Sanhedrin* of the *Talmud* it is said, "Seven days before the deluge, the Holy One changed the primeval order and the sun rose in the west and set in the east."

Certainly, if our planet's axis had been tilted, the sky would appear to have moved in relation to the earth.

FIRST CAME FIRE
Many of the Deluge legends report a Great Fire which swept over the earth as part of the Great Flood catastrophe.

A Babylonian version of the event says: "All the earth spirits leaped up with flaming torches, and with the brightness thereof they lit up the earth." Through high-speed photography, scientists have discovered that in some cases lightning does not come down to strike the earth, but is from the earth itself into the heavens.

Electrical discharges between the earth and sky probably lit up the heavens in this manner just before the Deluge began.

The Cato Indians of California relate that the first world was evil and needed re-creating. Accordingly, the mountains were set on fire.

The 'thundergod', who lives in the world above, extinguished the conflagration with a flood of hot water. Then it began to rain night and day until the water covered the earth.

A Brazilian flood tradition relates that Monan, the chief god, sent a fierce fire to burn up the world and its wicked people. Then a magician caused so much rain to fall in putting out the fire that the earth became flooded.

The volcanic activity generated by the sudden disruption of the earth's crust must have set fire to some of the massive forests. Today, some of the buried forests (now found as coal) show signs of fierce burning before they were buried.

The display of **lightning, volcanoes erupting** and **huge forests burning** must have been an awesome and frightening prelude to the Flood itself.

There was still no rain. But it would come.

2

The event itself (b) -
EXPLOSION FROM HELL

The kids were sent home early that afternoon. The headmaster called an emergency school assembly and told the pupils they should return home to be with their parents.

As it happened, they never returned to school. Never.

* * * * * * *

The same external force that tipped the earth over, generated high speed ultra-vibrations within the earth. It disrupted the designed balance within the earth, unleashing a literal thermonuclear meltdown. A chain of events began comparable to placing an egg in a micro-wave oven.[1]

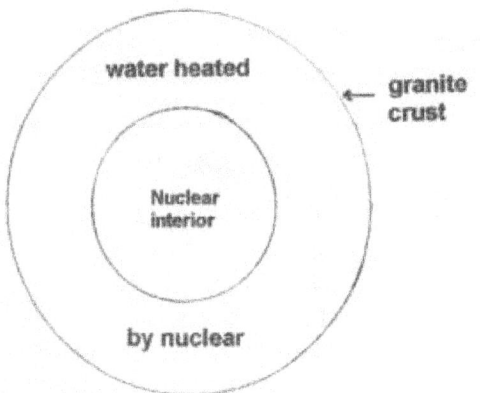

We noted in Book 1 (*The Killing of Paradise Planet*) that huge amounts of water were encased under the earth's granite crust. Now this water began heating rapidly, the heat adding to pressure, which added to heat, and more pressure. And in a matter of minutes something had to give.

The pressure build-up became enormous. And the earth's granite crust exploded.

The waters, under super-pressure, began to rip the earth apart at the seams.

A crack appears

At first, there appeared a microscopic crack, which grew in both directions. At the speed of about 2½ miles a second, following the path of least resistance, the crack began to move around the earth. It encircled the globe in about eight minutes.

Under great pressure, other cracks were opening up. As these great cracks joined, fire spat out of the earth.

In these brief eight minutes the earth was ripped into continents. They were not separated at this time, but simply ripped apart at the seams.

Eruptions would have begun where the granite crust was thinner, probably in the Pacific area.

EARTHQUAKES

With the sudden rupture of the granite crust, the stresses and friction would have been enormous.

The tilting of the earth's axis generated a devastating earthquake.

I have before me a work of great antiquity, the *Book of Jasher*. Its age is believed to be about 3,400 years. It purports to relate historical events preceding and following the Great Flood. The account states that the preliminary upheaval commenced about a week before the Flood. At this time "the Lord caused the whole earth to shake, and the sun darkened, and the foundations of the world raged, and the whole earth was moved violently, and the lightning flashed, and the thunder roared, and all the fountains in the earth were broken up, such as was not known to the inhabitants before."[2]

The earthquakes that ripped open the earth's surface were greater than anything we have experienced. Edward Suess, the noted Austrian geologist, says that they were "of such indescribable and overpowering violence that the imagination refuses to follow the understanding...."[3]

A modern, though faint, echo of this event occurred in Calabria in 1783. An earthquake "caused fissures to be opened 500 feet wide and a thousand feet long, and down them were precipitated men, women, and children, houses, churches, public buildings, and whole farms. Some of the gaping chasms closed again. Others remained open until nature slowly healed its scars."[4]

During the 1755 Lisbon earthquake, a wide fissure was torn open in Morocco and an entire town of 8,000 people was literally swallowed up.

From 1811 to 1812, an earthquake known as "the great earthquake in the West" occurred in the Mississippi Valley. It affected an area about 300 miles long. "The earth on the shores [of the river] opened in gaping fissures and, closing again, threw the water, sand and mud in huge jets higher than the tops of the trees...

"The change wrought in the topography in the stricken area was staggering... Hills had disappeared, and new lakes were found in their place.... Numerous lakes became elevated ground.... In other places upland forest regions dropped fifty to one hundred feet, forming awesome chasms or new lakes. One of the lakes thus formed was about seventy miles long and from three to twenty miles wide."[5]

Multiply these events a million times, with such scenes occurring in every part of the world, and you might be able to visualise the meaning of the few but pregnant words of Genesis: "and the fountains of the great deep WERE BROKEN UP".[6]

UNDERGROUND BASINS BURST FORTH

The original extent of this "great deep" is indicated by the depth of the disturbed layers of the earth today.

The earth's stratified layers are, on average, about half a mile (one kilometre) deep. Some oil fields which have filled these basins have a depth of over 3 miles, while the deepest sediment filling these holes has been measured at 10 miles (16 kilometres).

These basins, before the Big Event, were filled with vast amounts of water.

CANOPY COLLAPSES

Now, with the radioactive balance under the earth disturbed, violent energy was released. Vast amounts of water were suddenly heated to over 250 degrees Fahrenheit.

Under enormous pressure, the water exploded through the granite crust. It was expelled at such force that narrow jets shot 70 miles into the sky.

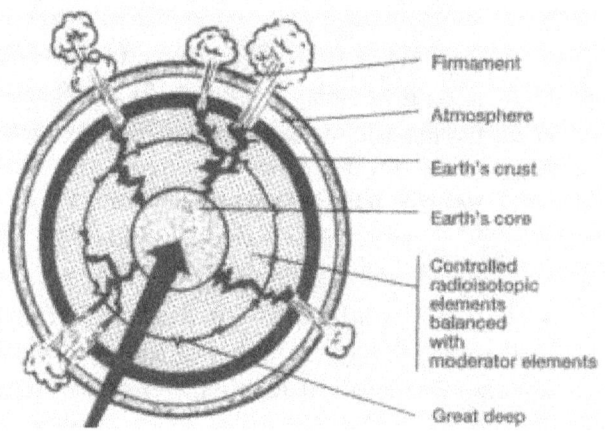

The puncturing of the canopy (Carl Baugh)

The first hot jets of water would have shot against the canopy. They ripped open holes or windows in the canopy. As Genesis puts it, "the windows of heaven were opened."[7]

The sides of those holes began to collapse.

Soon the entire outer canopy began to disintegrate.

The result: sudden, violent temperature changes. In certain areas, due to the lines of force at the earth's magnetic poles, the canopy would disintegrate as blocks of ice. But universally it would descend as rain.

The canopy began to collapse in great cataracts upon the earth. It poured down in such volume and force, the result was disastrous. This condensing mass of extra water made it possible for torrential rain to fall continuously over the entire earth for 40 days and nights.

It was at this time that these waters entered our present oceans.

Simultaneously, through the newly opened cracks in the earth's surface, poured molten rock, steam and water.

Ancient Mexican traditions of the event say that "the earth fell to pieces and the waters in its bosom uprushed with violence and overflowed."

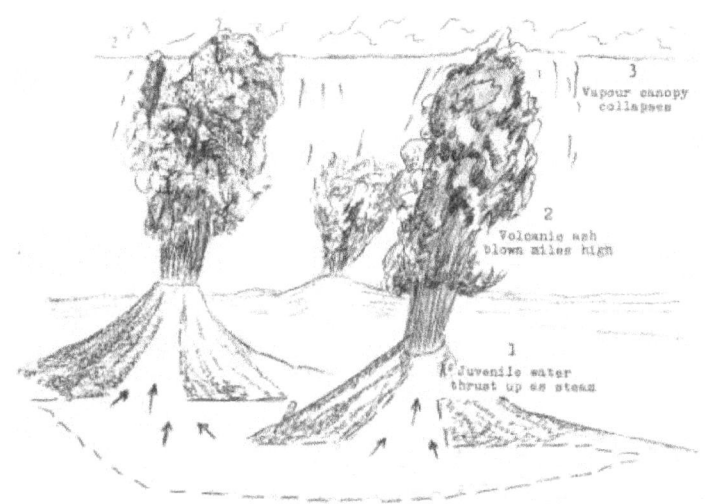

Colossal tidal waves

And since the daily rotation of the earth was now disturbed, the planet's waters were set into excessive tidal action. Moved by inertia, tidal waves rushed up over the land.

The water that would soon cover the earth was coming from three sources:
- the underground basins
- the firmament canopy
- and thousands of new volcanoes

VOLCANIC ACTION

The breaking up of the surface to a depth of several miles produced terrific strains and friction, which developed pent-up heat. Simultaneously, volcanoes burst out in America, Africa, the Pacific and everywhere. Lava not only spouted from craters, but also pushed upward from immense cracks in the crust.

With a roar, thousands of fiery columns spurted into the sky, sweeping up crackling pebbles, lava and masses of incandescent magma. Flames shot miles high.

Mighty showers of volcanic debris covered plant and animal life.

The forces of hell were let loose. Glowing, red-hot magma shot up at terrific speed and mixed with ocean waters. This created all the conditions for a submarine volcanic eruption of the greatest possible violence. Huge fracture seams were torn apart in a matter of days. Terrestrial fire and ocean water became embroiled in ever-increasing volume.

Today, marine strata coal beds often show evidence of this volcanic activity that occurred while the trees were being buried by the water.

And **modern volcanic eruptions** help us to visualise what happened back there.

When Mauna Loa, Hawaii, erupted in 1855, the lava ran over the land at 40 miles per hour, faster than a swift horse.

The explosion of Krakatoa on August 27, 1883, was so loud it was heard on the island of Rodriluez nearly 3,000 miles (4,800 kilometres) away. The eruption threw rocks 17 miles (28,000 metres) into the air, blew most of the 18 square mile island to pieces and left a hole in the ocean 1,000 feet deep. Shock waves circled the earth 7 times, affecting barometers everywhere and they were still being recorded a week later. The resulting ocean wave raced at 400 miles (640 kilometres) an hour, washing steamships miles inland. The eruption cloud rose 29 miles (150,000 feet). So dense was the dust that **for 100 miles (160 kilometres) around, the darkness of midnight prevailed at midday.**

YET THESE WERE MERE RIFLE SHOTS COMPARED TO THE DELUGE.

For days, weeks and months, an estimated 30,000 Krakatoas, Vesuviuses and Mount St. Helens, shook and tore at the foundation of the earth, roaring with incessant thunder, belching forth dust, steam, boulders and lava – and lighting up the darkened sky with their terrifying and lurid flames.[8]

This is not imagination. The rocks of our earth show that it happened.

For the first six weeks, lava poured out wildly **above** the rising flood level. Thereafter, volcanoes (now submerged) continued to force out lava beneath the water.

Meanwhile, the continual tidal waves produced an ebb and flow, laying down successive strata containing land and water forms, interbedded with layers of primitive minerals from the original crust. Today, volcanic rocks lie interbedded with water-laid sedimentary rocks of all supposed geological "ages". This is exactly what we should expect to find according to the Genesis implication that the "fountains of the great deep" continued to eject their contents throughout the entire Deluge period.[9]

Frank Marsh comments:

"The explosion of the earth's crust which shattered rock fragments everywhere is evidenced today by the abundance of rounded stones which we find along stream beds, on pebbly beaches, mixed with the soil of narrow valleys, and often in great quantities elsewhere. There is no other explanation for these rounded stones than that they are an abundance of shattered fragments being worn by water under great agitation. They are not being formed now except in very limited amounts. Waves do not form them; neither do streams. These agencies dissolve some rock substances and wear rock strata into sand, but do not form rounded stones. The Genesis picture of the Noachian Flood beginning with the shattering of the layers of the earth's crust and then the shaping of these fragments into spherical bodies furnishes us with the only adequate explanation possible."[10]

The 150 days of seething, ebb-flowing water were of the right magnitude and kind to accomplish these mysterious phenomena.

Typical among the thousands of volcanoes active during the Deluge was Mount Ararat in eastern Turkey. There is clear evidence that not only was it once covered by water, but that it erupted while submerged under great depths of water. Flood-laid sediment 14,000 feet up contains fossilised remains of ocean creatures. On the exposed north-eastern face, lava layers are intermixed with sediment layers. "Pillow lava" is found at 15,000 feet (as high up as rocks are exposed). This is **formed only** when the lava is spewed out **under great depths of water**.

And notice: "Pillow lava is probably the most abundant form of volcanic rock on earth."[11]

The result as seen today
Large areas of volcanic rock spread over Africa, India, the U.S.A., Iceland, Brazil, Argentina, the Baltic, Siberia and elsewhere.

India's 700,000 square mile Deccan Plateau is ten thousand feet thick! Lava 10,000 feet thick!
In Idaho, Oregon and Washington, U.S.A., are the remains of an enormous volcanic eruption. The Columbia Plateau covers 250,000 square miles. **The lava flow is up to 5,000 feet thick** in places.[12] The Seven Devils Canyon of Snake River has cut a channel over 3,000 feet deep into this.

"Only a few thousand years ago lava flowed there over an area larger than France, Switzerland, and Belgium combined; it flowed not as a creek, not as a river, not even as an overflowing stream, but as a flood, deluging horizon after horizon, filling all the valleys, devouring all the forests and habitations, steaming large lakes out of existence as they were little potholes filled with water, swelling ever higher and overtopping mountains and burying them deep beneath molten stone, boiling and bubbling, thousands of feet thick, billions of tons heavy."[13]

At Nampa, Idaho, in 1889, during the boring of an artesian well on this plateau, a small figurine was brought up from a depth of 320 feet – evidence of human activity before the disaster struck.

The Canadian Shield comprises 2,000,000 square miles of lava flow. Only a tremendous catastrophe could cause such an eruption. Nothing today compares with this.

From Lebanon almost to South Africa's Cape runs a mighty rift – a zone which shows a tearing apart of the crust, produced by a direct tension. It covers about one sixth of the planet's circumference. Concerning this, Gregory wrote: "**It must have some worldwide cause.**"[14]   Indeed!   The geologist Eduard Suess observed that **immense floods** of lava gushed from the earth along the Rift. Vigorous volcanic action was generated.

In many places the bottom of the sea consists of a lava bed covered only by a thin veneer of sediment. The Indian Ocean is largely circled with extinct volcanoes; the ocean bottom is of lava. This is true also of the Atlantic and Pacific.

Most of the oceanic islands, both above and below sea level, were primarily of volcanic origin.

All of the world's huge flows, flowing like seas of lava, seem to have come from rifts in the crust. This is NOT NORMAL volcanism, but **HAS THE FLAVOUR OF CATASTROPHE**. These rifts seem to be huge tears in the crust of the planet, from which lava poured like a flood.

Nothing seen in recognised historical times can compare with whatever catastrophe caused these tremendous formations. The theory of uniformity breaks down completely in the face of this undeniable catastrophe.

THE CONNECTION WITH THE GREAT FLOOD

Sometimes, this question is asked concerning the Great Flood: "How could clouds form fast enough and continue to form and to produce sufficient water for rain non-stop for six weeks – as the Bible claims? What produced the necessary evaporation?"

First, let's understand that even today, there are areas in the tropics where rain **never ceases**. In one continuous rainy season, it falls without interruption day after day, year in and year out. This is all through the normal process of evaporation and rainfall; an unbelievable quantity of water circulates there between the earth and sky. This is under perfectly normal conditions.

But with the Great Flood, other factors were in play:
1. **The collapse of the firmament canopy.**
2. **An abrupt change in climate** came with the Deluge.
   The impact of this sudden change must have been terrific. As cold air met the warm, mountains of fog and cloud rose into the air, and then fell back in the form of torrential rains.
3. **The volcanoes themselves** caused rain on an unprecedented scale.

The gaseous products of volcanoes consist of 80 percent water vapour, 10 percent carbon dioxide and 10 percent other gases.

In fact, when volcanoes erupt, as much as 20 percent of all the erupted material is water! This water comes from deep beneath the earth's crust. It has been under very high pressure, therefore its temperature is extremely hot. It soars into the atmosphere as steam and soon condenses as rain.

This water has never been on the surface of the earth before, so it is called **juvenile water**. Each time a volcano erupts, more water is added to the oceans – water that was never there before.

Granite magma can hold six to nine percent water in solution.[15]

Volcanoes give off vapour in quantities almost beyond comprehension. Take a few modern examples:

Mount Etna, in Sicily. In just 100 days, steam equivalent to 460 million gallons of water issued from one of the subsidiary cones. That was 4,600,000 gallons a day from only a **secondary** cone of one volcano.

Data from the Mexican volcano Paricutin suggests that between 1943 and 1952, the period of its most active life, it may have expelled juvenile water equivalent to about 6 kilometres square by one metre deep!

Imagine several thousand volcanoes in furious activity all over the earth and in the seas, and the cloud-forming possibilities at once appear as beyond calculation.

The sea also began to rise. Each twice-daily current came higher and higher up the rivers and valleys, spreading further and wider inland each time; then it would recede. The incoming movements must have been fierce and violent, progressively tearing at the land and whisking it away.

Pima Indian legends mention that the advancing waters were cut by incessant lightning.

The ancient *Popul Vuh* of the Quiche of Guatemala paints a vivid picture of men caught in the advancing Great Flood.

"There came a great flood, followed by a thick rain of bitumen and resin, when men ran, here and there, in despair and madness. They tried, beside themselves with terror, to climb on the roofs of houses, which crumbled and threw them to the ground. Trees they tried to ascend, which threw them far away. They sought to enter caves and grottoes and immediately they were shut in from the exterior. The earth darkened and it rained night and day. Thus was accomplished the ruin of the race of man which was given up to destruction."

Special note

In our book *The Killing of Paradise Planet*, we suggested that originally Planet Earth was surrounded by a compressed hydrogen canopy stretched out 11 miles above the earth. This diffused incoming solar heat equally to provide a moderate warm climate from pole to pole.

We also noted that below the solid granite crust of the earth were massive reservoirs of water, as well as huge piles of asphalt and oil in the original hydrocarbon form. Likewise, the radio-isotopic elements below ground were perfectly balanced.

A fascinating scenario has been proposed by Dr. Carl Baugh of Glen Rose, Texas. He has likened the composition of this original earth to that of an egg.

Put an egg into a micro-wave (please don't!), push the button, and the egg will literally explode! Baugh then reminds us of an ancient scripture (Psalm 46:6) which states that the Creator "uttered his voice – and the earth melted". And he asks, "What is voice, but energy waves?" With the simple statement, "I have had enough," the Creator could have done it with His voice.

Such an energy wave would have caused something similar to the atomic melting that occurred at Chernobyl in Russia – a meltdown within a thermonuclear context. Physicists do not even like to speak of a meltdown, because it is a catastrophic condition completely out of control. The scenario suggested is this:

"The earth's internal elements, including the radioisotopic elements, were in perfect balance. If these elements were unbalanced, or scattered, there was a grave consequence. But it appears that this is exactly what happened, and there was a resulting thermonuclear meltdown....

"Microwave energy is simply vibrations at two and a half billion times per second. Our voice is a vibratory form of energy, but we do not have the energy, or the power, or the ability, to vibrate our voice two and a half billion times per second."

Suppose the Creator, by his very nature all-powerful, simply said, "I have had enough." His voice could accomplish such a microwave reaction, suggests Baugh.

"When you push a button on your microwave oven, there is no heat – simply vibratory energy. That microwave energy traps the water molecules, because the water molecule is approximately the same dimension as the vibration spectrum. The microwave energy traps the water molecules and heats them up.

"Dr. Walter T. Brown entered this basic model in a computer, and he discovered that when the water was heated to two hundred and fifty degrees Fahrenheit, certain things would begin to happen. Dr. Brown found, as in the case of the egg, when water encased in the earth is heated to two hundred and fifty degrees, that heat adds to pressure, more pressure adds to heat, more heat adds to pressure, etc., and in a matter of minutes, something has to give. In the computer model, it became evident that **where the granite crust of the earth was thinner, eruptions would have begun, probably in the Pacific area.**

"If you were to photograph, at rapid shutter speed, an egg rupturing under microwave energy, you could see it in the picture being torn apart at the seams. The egg would be blown apart in small pieces and larger pieces, as in the case with the earth – continents and islands. Dr. Brown postulated from his computer model that **the ripping apart of the earth at the seams before the Flood would have occurred at two and one-half miles per second.** He found that it would have taken only **eight minutes to rip the earth into continents. They would not have been separated at this time,** but simply ripped apart at the seams.

"Dr Brown also found that the computer analysis revealed that **when the earth ruptured, water** would have been expunged in **a narrow band of jet streams with such force it would have erupted seventy miles high.**"[16]

So here is the possible mechanism of events:

The ancient writer says, "God uttered his **voice** [= energy waves] and the **earth melted**".

In modern terms, we might say that this microwave energy that struck the earth upset the interior nuclear balance. And this triggered a thermonuclear reaction inside the earth.

The result was devastating.

3

The event itself (c) -
WAVES AS FAST AS JET PLANES

...Three weeks have gone now.

The populations of the seacoasts are gone. Huge tidal waves are now sweeping inland. Nothing is alive for 600 miles inland. The survivors are dwellers in the centre of the continent. By day, the sky is now permanently darkened; the sun no longer shines. The moon cannot be seen.

Like a cosmic mower, the continuing hurricane cuts through forests, ruthlessly harvesting. And everywhere it goes, the hurricane hurls a lethal barrage of flying missiles - tree limbs, broken glass, whole roofs. Steel poles are twisted like spaghetti. The hurricanes and wild seas tear the trees from the ground and pile them, trunk, root and branch, in enormous heaps.

Gigantic waves sweep madly over valley and mountain alike, carrying rocks, stones and rubbish at enormous speed.

Each twice-daily current of the sea comes higher and higher up the rivers and valleys, spreading further and wider inland each time. It progressively tears at the land and whisks it away.

* * * * * * *

The Flood waters continued to rise for six weeks. The wind rapidly increased in fury, exploding into something unimaginable.

SURGING WAVES

Colossal waves, caused by submarine earthquakes, surged over the planet. The winds, now of immeasurable force, whipped them up to enormous heights.

This was not a calm, monotonous rise of water, but rather a mighty, turbulent upheaval. We are dealing with water the violence of which defies the imagination.

This was a flood of global proportions. All the latent forces of nature were unleashed. Earthquakes, volcanoes, wind and water, formed a terrible alliance for a universal destruction. The volume of the water was so great, and so disturbed by great upheavals, that it became a force sufficiently cosmic in proportion to accomplish most or all of the changes seen to the earth's surface, that some people have attributed to moving ice.

The combined action of volcanoes, earthquakes and great storms created POWER FOR DESTRUCTION AND TRANSPORTATION that is beyond human calculation.

The waters remained at their peak for a further 110 days. Even then, they were not in a state of quiet, but continued to plow and to move the materials of the earth's surface. The seas remained chaotic, crisscrossed by mighty fast-flowing tsunamis.

The power of the waves

In innumerable parts of the world (including isolated islands in the Pacific and Atlantic, as well as Antarctica), large boulders are found in a position which shows that a great force must have lifted them up and carried them long distances. Sometimes lying loose on local rocks of a different composition, these boulders are akin to formations far away in a foreign locality. Thus a granite boulder of foreign origin may perch on top of a high ridge of dolerite. Some great force brought it from afar.

In North America, for example, the Madison boulder near Conway, New Hampshire, measures 90 by 40 by 38 feet, and weighs almost 10,000 tons, about as much as the weight of 130,000 people! Unlike the bedrock beneath, it is composed of granite. Thus the boulder is called "erratic".[1]

On the shore and highlands of the British Isles and Germany are found enormous quantities of such boulders brought across the sea from Norway.

Boulders from Finland have been swept over Poland, the site of Moscow, and as far as the River Don. Often they are frighteningly piled up.

Huge blocks from Canada and Labrador lie strewn over North America. Some are plain GIGANTIC.

An erratic boulder in Warren County, Ohio, covers ¾ acre and weighs 13,500 tons (the load of a large cargo ship).

Two pieces of quartzite 30 miles south of Calgary, Alberta, are over 18,000 tons.[2]

Near Malmo, southern Sweden, is a mass of chalk stone 1,000 feet wide, up to 200 feet thick and THREE MILES (5 KILOMETRES) LONG![3]

One on England's east coast was so huge, a village had been unwittingly built on it.[4]

Carried by ice?

Could these erratic boulders have been **carried by ice? Definitely not**! Observations in the Alps have shown that glaciers carry stones downhill, not uphill.

"Erratic bounders are found in places where continental ice
could hardly have deposited them… on the Azores, islands
separated from the ice cover by a wide expanse of ocean."[5]

On the Isle of Man, in the Irish Sea, they are found near the summit, where **only waters** could have lifted them.

In Labrador, erratic bounders are rammed against the slopes of hills, something that only a tidal wave or tsunami could have done.

The fact that many were swept from the equator to the higher latitudes, is another problem for the ice theory.

Such boulders were broken off mountains far away, mountains under stress, mountains shattered by earthquakes, or heated and split by volcanic action.

In Europe, huge rocks thousands of cubic feet in size (one of them 10,000 cubic feet), were carried from the Alps, across a space now occupied by Lake Geneva, and hurled 2,000 feet up on to the Jura Mountains, where they still sit!

As says Horace Benedict de Saussure, eminent Swiss naturalist:

"This mass, shoved along by the onrush of great waters,
was left spread up the slopes where we still see many
scattered fragments."[6]

In some places, as in the Berkshires, England, erratic boulders are distributed in a long string.

In countless places worldwide, including China, Antarctica and isolated islands of the Pacific and Atlantic, lie erratics, brought from afar by enormous force. Broken off from the parent rock, they were carried over valleys and hills, over land and sea.[7]

The faster water moves, the more it can erode, the more it can lift.

If water increases in velocity by 4 times, it can transport not 4 but 54 times as much matter.

If it accelerates 100 times, it will carry **50 million** times as much material.

The immense striking power of a wave is evidenced frequently in our time.

In a December gale on America's Oregon coast, waves picked up a 135 pound rock and heaved it through the air, knocking a 20 foot hole in the roof of the Tillamook Lighthouse keeper's house 100 feet (ten stories in height) above the sea.

At Wicks, Scotland, waves swept from the breakwater a solid block of concrete weighing 2,600 tons.

Waves striking the shore of Tierra del Fuego can be heard for twenty miles.

"The force of waves striking the shore can be measured, and has been found to reach three tons per square foot."[8]

The speed of waves

In 1946, a tsunami from an Aleutian Island earthquake travelled 470 miles per hour across the Pacific.[9]

In 1960, Chilean earthquakes sent waves travelling at jet speeds of 525 miles an hour (840 kilometres per hour). As they hit Japan a third of the way around the world, the waves were still as high as a three storey building.[10]

The height of waves

The huge waves caused by seismic disturbances have been known to reach skyscraper heights.

On April 24, 1971, a wave off Ishigaki Island, Ryukyu Chain, was estimated at 278 feet high. This giant wave tossed a 750 ton block of coral more than 1.3 miles.

On May 18, 1980, an earthquake occurred directly under Mount St. Helens. As a result of the ensuing landslide into Spirit Lake, a giant water wave (or waves) up to 860 feet (262 metres) high scoured the north sides of the lake.

According to Guinness, on December 4, 1984, evidence was reported of an ancient ocean wave breaking on the southern shore of Lanai in the Hawaiian Islands. This wave was 1,000 feet high.[11]

In 1958, an earthquake in Alaska raised seismic waves more than 1,200 feet high.

On July 9, 1958, a landslip sent a wave to wash 1,740 feet high along the fjord-like Lituya Bay, Alaska.

John Strong calculates that there is no reason why, given gravitational interaction with an outside force, there could not be tides of 10,000 feet instead of 10 feet.

He suggests that "if a planet, that was disturbed in the outer regions of our solar system, began its fall to the sun and came into temporary capture by the earth, there would be a gravitational attraction on the water, dragging it to one side facing the visitor."

Of course, the earth would continue to spin, while the outside force produced a gravitational attraction on the water. The water would thus maintain its position facing the gravitational pull of the "visitor," while the earth turned beneath it.

This would produce a huge tide on that side of the earth – a tide perhaps 10,000 feet high, flowing over the continents once a day at about 1,000 miles per hour at the equator.[12]

We don't know whether additional factors augmented those already mentioned. However, Robert Dietz, writing in *Scientific American*, makes an interesting observation:

"A giant meteorite falling into the middle of the [North] Atlantic Ocean could generate a wave 20,000 feet high that would overwhelm vast areas of the continents surrounding [that] ocean, sweeping over the entire eastern seaboard of the United States and across the Appalachians."[13]

If you have access to a certain back copy of *Analog* (you may find it in your local library – look through its cumulative index. It is an issue that came out sometime before 1972), look for an article by J.E. Enever, entitled *"Giant Meteor Impact"*. Although this is a science fiction magazine, and this article is presented as fiction, it does give in simple language the true scientific mechanics of 20,000 foot waves.

Again, consider the power in such water

Even in today's relatively small floods, we see bridges, houses, trees and immense boulders ripped up and swept along like mere pebbles and matchsticks. Such floods seldom rise higher than a few dozen feet. Their main force is exhausted in days or hours.

But when we begin to speak in terms of a Flood that "grew mightily upon the earth" and "prevailed upon the earth one hundred and fifty days" and covered "all the high mountains which are under all the heavens", we must face the fact that we are no longer dealing with phenomena that are familiar to modern science.

In such a Flood we must therefore expect damage that staggers the imagination. Erosion and sedimentation must have taken place on a gigantic scale. Along with all the forces so far described, there must have been a great complexity of hydraulic phenomena, including cross-currents and whirlpools.

THE FLOOD **CAN EXPLAIN** MANY OTHERWISE PUZZLING GEOLOGICAL FEATURES OF TODAY'S EARTH.

As Immanuel Velikovsky observes, "Billows miles high travelled over the land."[14]

That this event occurred just a few thousand years ago can be established by the extent to which the rocks under the erratic boulders are denuded. Speaking, for example, of Wales and Yorkshire, Upham testifies that the amount of denudation of limestone rocks on which bounders lie" is a "proof that a period of no more than six thousand years has elapsed since the boulders were left in their positions."[15]

You won't find a great deal written about this today. It is dangerous information... an embarrassment to the established teachings.

Because, firstly, this event was GLOBAL.

And secondly, it was "RECENT" – more recent than any mainstream dating system allows for.

And now comes more explosive information. It may not sound very important, at first. But you'll soon see HOW important this is.

We shall now discover WHY the same kinds of fossils are often found in groups, in the earth's strata. And also WHY these groups do tend to be found in a certain order.

It's not what you think.

THE PHYSICAL FORCES IN THE DELUGE - Summary

AXIS TILTED
No phenomenon on earth is adequate to displace the earth's axis; it could be caused only by some **outside** force. The earth's axis **was** tilted – and **suddenly** – bringing terrific stresses upon the earth's surface, and total destruction.

EARTHQUAKES
Earthquakes tore the crust into gigantic fissures, to pour forth water, steam and molten rock.

UNDERGROUND BASINS BURST FORTH
As untold amounts of primary water broke free, they rushed out over the earth in a great swell. The sea began to overflow, sweeping inland, tearing away the land.

VOLCANIC ACTION
The breaking of the surface to a depth of several miles produced terrific strains and friction, which developed pent-up heat. Simultaneously, volcanoes burst out in America, Africa, the Pacific and everywhere else. With a roar, thirty thousand fiery columns spouted miles high into the sky. Lava also pushed upward from immense cracks in the crust. The volcanoes gave off vapour in quantities almost beyond comprehension, causing great rain on an unprecedented scale.

CANOPY COLLAPSED
The sudden tilting of the planet's axis and the expulsion of jets of boiling water and of volcanic ash high above the atmosphere disrupted the vast amounts of invisible water in the canopy surrounding the planet. This outer canopy began to disintegrate, to collapse upon the earth. It poured down in such volume and force, the result was disastrous.

TIDAL WAVES

This was not a calm, monotonous rise of water. Colossal tidal waves surged over the planet. The winds, now of uncontrollable force, whipped them to enormous heights. Boulders of up to 18,000 tons were carried hundreds of miles. Some were hurled to levels 2,000 feet higher.

GLOBAL

This was a Flood of global proportions. All the latent forces of nature – volcanoes, earthquakes, waves and hurricanes – were unleashed in a terrible alliance for a universal destruction. For a year, their continued action created power for destruction and transportation that is beyond human calculation. Erosion and sedimentation took place on a gigantic scale.

THE FLOOD CAN EXPLAIN MANY OTHERWISE PUZZLING GEOLOGICAL FEATURES OF TODAY'S EARTH.

4

The event itself (d) -
STAMPEDE

"Senor, look at this…"
He pushed the leaves aside and pointed.
"A stalk… Just a broken stalk."
"No," he exclaimed, glaring at me as though I were dumb. "A jaguar."

* * * * * * *

In the largely un-explored Amazon headwaters we were pushing our way through what appeared to be trackless, thick undergrowth. So dense that one would be hard pressed to hear a river ten feet away. It absorbed all sound. Just four of us – an Ecuadorian half-caste, two native carriers and myself, were trekking east to who knows where? We were probably off the map by now. This was an unknown world of ferocious insects, fierce jungle beasts and fiercer men. We were somewhere in "head-shrinking" country.

Yuka, the squat, red-skinned carrier, traced the ground near the broken leaf. Whatever his trained eye saw, it was invisible to me.

"She came past yesterday. A female. She had a cub with her."

My admiration for his skills soared dramatically. In a jungle with no "tracks", this five foot man could guide us anywhere – even back to safety, if he chose.

FOOTPRINTS. That's what I'm talking about. Experts read them like a note. You can tell who left them. Indeed, much more than that, as we shall see.

On the south side of the Grand Canyon in Arizona is an old trail leading into a side canyon. Part way along, it passes among blocks of sandstone that have footprints of animals on them. **These footprints are all going uphill.** (The same is true of footprints seen in many other parts of the south western U.S.A.)

39

An experiment with lizards conducted by Dr. Leonard Brand of Loma Linda University, California, showed that on **dry** land these animals do **not** leave clear tracks. On sand under or along the edge of **water**, footprints left are sharp and clear, most like the fossil prints.

Apparently, the fossil tracks were **made under strange conditions. Going uphill, while on the edge of or under water!**

Why would animals that were leaving footprints in the sand long ago all be walking uphill? Were these animals trying to escape from rising flood water?

Leaving tracks as perhaps they fled from the rising water, the animals were later drowned and their bodies washed away, not to sink down and suffer burial until later. Usually the tracks were covered with many feet of sand and mud before the bodies were covered.

WHY "SIMPLER" FOSSILS ARE SOMETIMES LOWER DOWN

The remains of animals, as well as their tracks, are called fossils. Interestingly, the simpler creatures are sometimes found buried lower down and the more complex animals higher up in the layers of sediment. This sequence has been used to support the theory of evolution. From simple organisms, we are told, life has ascended over vast ages to more complex forms.

Yes, there are places where you find fossils laid out (to a limited extent) like the table in the geology book. And it looks convincing.

Fossils often in groups

In the rock strata fossils do tend to be found in groups. What is more, these groups do tend to be found in a certain order. For example, Cambrian trilobites and Cretaceous dinosaurs are not usually found together. Why is this?

According to evolution theory, the trilobites died out long before the dinosaurs lived.

But could there be another, more natural explanation?

Suppose both trilobites and dinosaurs were alive today. They certainly would not be found together, since they would live and die in different localities and environments.

Is it possible that the order of the fossils is not the record of ascending evolution at all, but simply the record of animals trapped in particular environments when the Flood overtook them?

Because animals and plants live in different areas, they would have been trapped in sediments representative of their particular environment.

The Flood by its very nature was a chaotic and disorderly event. For this reason, there would be many exceptions, but the order of fossils now seen would be the usual order of burial.

Could it be, then, that the order of fossils is not the record of ascending evolution at all, but simply the way the Flood waters sorted them out and laid them down?

Natural laws were in operation. Let's notice these.

1. **Habitat and mobility**

    First the lowest creatures inhabiting the deep ocean were overwhelmed and buried. Many of them – like the brachiopods, crinoids, trilobites and oysters – were more or less fastened to the bottom, and thus were helpless and easily buried by the disturbance of the waters.

    These waters and disturbed sediments then overtook the amphibians and land-bordering creatures.

    As the Flood waters advanced, the swamp, marsh and low river-flat creatures were overtaken, including, notably, reptiles.

    Most land animals and humans, with their greater mobility, were able to escape temporarily to higher ground as the waters rose. Occasionally, however, individuals were swept away and entombed in the sediments. But eventually, even those who had escaped to the highest elevations were overtaken.

    In many places, groups of animals which had huddled near caves or on hillsides were swept away en masse by a sudden sediment-laden wave to be buried together at another place.

    In most cases men were not buried but simply drowned, their bodies borne on or near the water surface until finally decomposed. This accounts for the rarity of human fossils.

    Birds also, due to their superior mobility and light weight, would be at or near the surface, where they would decay rather than becoming fossilised. This is why birds are not common in the fossil record.

The general order of buried fossils (from simple on the bottom to complex on top) is thus exactly what would be expected in such a catastrophe. The Flood would in general have tended to form just such strata in the order that geologists expect, when they look for geological "ages". Simple marine life tends to be found in the lower elevations of rock, simply because they lived at the lowest elevations.

The various "ages" are not "ages" at all, but are actually DIFFERENT ECOLOGICAL ZONES OF THE SAME ERA – the Flood era.

2. **Specific gravity**

Density and shape also had a great deal to do with the depth at which various creatures were buried.

All shellfish are heavy and float less readily. Trilobites, which are not only heavy, but quite spherical (streamlined), would settle out quickly and tend to be found in the deepest, so-called Cambrian, strata.

On the other hand, the partially decayed body of a man or a mammal becomes distended with gases and can hardly be made to sink. Then again, the more complex creatures are also less spherical and dense, causing them to be buried higher in the sediment.

3. **The sorting action of water**

Later during the Flood year, the retreating waters reworked and redeposited some of the strata. This sorting action of the moving water naturally separated both organic and inorganic particles into collections of similar sizes and shapes.

During the first few months of the Flood, the dead animals would settle out in great swirling piles, as the water swirled around – and this would cause the massive fossil graveyards. The plants would pack and get buried, to turn to coal.

Such sifting action of water can be seen on most beaches, where one finds big rocks and logs on higher ground, while moving on down there are smaller rocks, and then sand. Of course this action is not perfect. Usually there is some mixing of the materials, and sometimes a great deal.

HOW THE FLOOD WATERS OVERTOOK FLEEING ANIMALS

The decrease in shell thickness of dinosaur eggs as one moves up through the strata (discovered in a number of regions by Heinrich Erben of the Bonn University of Paleontology) testifies to **the increasing stress as the dinosaurs struggled to higher ground**.

(Studies of birds show that stress can upset the animal's hormone balance and affect the amount of calcium deposited in egg shells.)

As conditions worsened, the reptiles laid eggs with thinner walls and the calcium supply decreased.

Fossilised tracks of animals show that in most cases the animals were not wading or loitering about; **they were fleeing**. The form of the footprints show that an animal was indecisive, a normal reaction if it was trapped by some peril closing in from all sides. Possibly within minutes of making these tracks, the fleeing animals were overwhelmed.

Gripped by the same terror, wild beasts and tame creatures stampeded to save their lives. In a common fear, their mutual animosity was lost.

One can see the terrified and panic-stricken beasts struggling to higher grounds and to hilltops before the onrushing flood. The lion took no heed of the lamb, nor the wolf of the hare. All were bent on saving their own lives.

Then they found themselves trapped in amphitheatres in the hills. In great numbers they thronged together, pushing into caves, swarming over the ground in front.

Until the waters rose and covered them. Strong animals, without a sign of degeneration, came to an end. This was not the survival of the fittest. "Fit and unfit, and mostly fit, old and young with sharp teeth, with strong muscles, with fleet legs, with plenty of food around, all perished."[1]

The earth was even at this moment convulsing, opening up fissures to swallow many of them, as they collected on the tops of these hills.

Then the huge waves smashed over them large rocks and debris, until their bones were crushed and smashed. So the bones of the large and small, the gentle and ferocious, were thrown together in wild confusion in a common grave, preserved for a memorial and a warning.

Elsewhere, animals of all kinds were swept along in the currents, their bones dashed within their bodies into thousands of fragments, eventually to be sorted by local currents and washed into crevices and held tight.

Worldwide, racial traditions recount this terrifying disaster, with its enormous universal rains, violent waterspouts, earthquakes and hurricane winds. The agonised cries of drowning men and beasts piercing the air. The terror-stricken dash by man and animal alike to reach the safety of mountains – and even of the great ship – only to be sucked under by the relentless force of turbulent waters.

Those that were left had been reduced to a state where they were little more than terrified animals. They never knew whether another violent flow of hot lava would open up beside them, an earthquake might swallow them up, or whether the rising waters would get them first.

At last man, the chief object of the waters, was overtaken. Outside the survival vessel, man ceased to exist. The destruction was complete – and sudden.

High tides and hurricanes now rushed from pole to pole. The enticing beauty of the antediluvian world had perished.

The waters continue to increase

Genesis 7:11-24 speaks of this great catastrophe taking 150 days for the Flood to reach its maximum height. It has actually been proposed by some that if the earth was suddenly tilted on its axis 23½ degrees or more, such a tilt could cause tidal waves to sweep around the earth twice a day and reach their maximum height in 150 days.

Is this what is meant in Genesis 8:3-5?

The same account describes events as witnessed by the survivors. In Book One of this 3-part series, *The Killing of Paradise Planet*, we dug deeply into numerous questions concerning the survivors of such a cataclysm, as well as their means of survival, the legendary "Ark". So we shall not cover these here.

However, the ancient Genesis record continues thus:

"And the waters mounted and lifted up the ark and it went along high above the earth. The waters grew mighty and mounted greatly over the earth and the ark floated upon the face of the waters. But the waters grew extremely mighty upon the earth, and all the high mountains which are under all the heavens were covered." "...upwards did the waters grow mightily so that the mountains were covered."[2]

From the choice of words and by the repetition of expressions, it becomes evident that there was enormous power in the surging, raging waters. The earth's surface was plowed up ten miles in some spots and overall to an average depth of almost a mile.

These titanic waves, driven by screaming gusts, continued to rise. After 40 days, the waters were above the highest mountains. (Although some thousands of feet, the antediluvian mountains were not the giants of today. Peaks like Everest were not pushed up until later in the Flood and the early post-Flood aftermath.)

Half a year was to pass before the tops of the mountains would again be seen.[3]

Meanwhile, vast geological changes were occurring.

Amid such titanic forces, only a miracle could have preserved the Ark. "Fifteen cubits and upwards did the waters prevail," that is, the survival vessel sank into the water to a depth of fifteen cubits, half its total height, when fully laden – while floating over the mountains.

For months longer, the storm raged. Unceasingly, in repeating twelve hour cycles, the mighty ebb and flow wore down the earth's surface. And each next wave returned with its debris. Travelling long distances under water, fast moving currents of suspended mud and sand spread out over thousands of square miles. The ebb and flow laid down successive strata, alternately burying land organisms and water creatures, which would ultimately fossilise.

Volcanoes intensified under the surface.

As well as laying down strata, the Flood sorted debris into piles here and there. The sedimentation of today's rivers collects in the eddies and bays and is there deposited in much the same way that a universal Flood would have deposited specimens together from various other locations.

* * * * * * *

As this Great Disaster progresses, I want to take you on a world tour... to France, Gibraltar, the Middle East. And just see what this event is doing to our planet... and its inhabitants.

Good, solid evidence you will see. Of the kind to make your flesh creep...

5

Fissures of Bones (a) -
UNNATURAL GRAVEYARDS

Gripped by the same terror, wild beasts and tame struggle together to higher grounds.

Some of the people bind their children and themselves upon powerful animals, knowing that these will climb to the highest peaks to escape the rising waters.

Some fasten themselves to tall trees on the hills or mountains, but the trees are uprooted and hurled into the billows.

As the waters rise higher, the people flee for refuge to the loftiest heights. Often man and beast struggle together for a foothold... in the blinding rain.

In amphitheatres in the hills, they find themselves trapped. In great numbers they throng together, pushing into caves, swarming over the ground in front.

Until the waters rise and cover them. Strong animals, without a sign of degeneration, come to an end. This is not the survival of the fittest. Fit and unfit, and mostly fit, old and young with sharp teeth, with strong muscles, with fleet legs, with plenty of food around, all perish.

The earth is even at this moment convulsing, opening up fissures to swallow many of them, as they collect on the tops of these hills. Then the huge waves smash over them large rocks and debris, until their bones are crushed and smashed. Here, often thousands of feet up, they are washed into crevices and held tight.

* * * * * * *

Just in case you are not aware, here is an intriguing fact.

When in great panic, flesh-eating animals and the animals that are usually their prey, flee together. They do not attack each other or fear each other. All gripped by the same terror, they pay no attention to one another.

Their mutual animosity is lost in a common fear.

There is a most crucial circumstance concerning the earth's strata and the fossils that is not generally disclosed to the public, and which many geologists apparently do not recognise.

On every continent, and in numerous places on each, are vast "fossil graveyards", where masses of flora and fauna have been swept to a sudden death in their millions.

These areas are often packed with both land and sea creatures from different habitats and even different climatic zones – all mixed and buried together **in a completely unnatural way**.

There is evidence that a great disaster took place, in which creatures of all types perished together – mostly fit, young and old, with fleet legs, strong muscles and sharp teeth. And with plenty of food around. Artifacts of man are found among them.

They all died together, suddenly and violently, high up on hills and mountains.

What did it?

Come with me on a global tour. You'll see what I mean.

France

In the Mediterranean coastal area of France, numerous clefts crammed to overflowing with animal bones have been found. Along with them are human remains.

One could mention Mount Genay, near Semur in Burgundy – 1,430 feet high. Here, capped by a breccia (a cemented mass of stone fragments), is a fissure filled with mixed bones of numerous animals.

Near Chalon-sur-Saone, between Dijon and Lyons, stands an isolated hill, flat-topped Mont de Sautenay. It rises 1,030 feet above the plain. Near the summit is a fissure crammed with bones. The bones are unweathered and ungnawed.

Albert Gaudry, professor at the Jardin des Plantes, asks:

"Why should so many wolves, bears, horses and oxen have ascended a hill isolated on all sides?" These broken and splintered bones are "evidently not those of animals devoured by beasts of prey; nor have they been broken by man. Nevertheless the remains of wolf were particularly abundant, together with those of cave lion, bear, rhinoceros, horse, ox and deer. It is not possible to suppose that animals of such different natures, and of such different habitats, would in life ever have been together."[1]

Velikovsky directs us to note that "the state of preservation of the bones indicates that the animals – all of them – perished in the same period of time."[2]

Prestwich concluded that the bones were "now associated in the fissure on the summit of the hill" because "all these animals had fled (there) to escape the rising waters."[3]

Caves and fissures on the Cote d'Azur have yielded mixed land and sea remains. For example, in the Vallonet cave at Roquebrune-Cap-Martin, between Monaco and the Italian border, were bones of lions, rhinoceros, hyenas, macao monkeys, elephants and **whales**. All together.[4]

Britain

In Holderness, Yorkshire, bones of seals and walrus (from cooler latitudes) are lumped together with fresh-water molluscs of warm climate – and in similar strata are hippopotami.

Near Plymouth, clefts in the rock are filled with bones of rhinoceros, polar bear, hippopotamus, mammoth, bison, horse, wolf, lion, hyena and bear. They are broken into fragments. All are mixed up with other animals' bones. There is not one entire skeleton. The bones, showing neither wear nor gnawing by beasts of prey, are intermingled with rock fragments.

Remains are found in similar condition in Devonshire and in Pembrokeshire, Wales. The bones are broken and splintered, in a "fresh state", with no trace of weathering.

Significantly, one of the foremost investigators of the Cefn caves in Wales concluded that they had been "submerged".[5]

A **marine** invasion has also been postulated to account for the remains at Cae Gwyn, near Denbigh.[6]

Similar discoveries in Eire are likewise attributed to water action.[7]

In various places "forest beds" have been found. But the roots are broken off, in most cases one to three feet from the trunk. They are recognised as having drifted".[8]

The Norfolk forest bed contains bones of 60 species of large and small mammals, including tigers, bears, elephants, hippopotamus and horse, as well as an assortment of smaller creatures, from arctic, temperate and tropical regions. Immediately over the forest bed are arctic plants and shells. The mollusc shells are found in the position of life, with closed valves. They did not die a natural death, but were buried alive.

Velikovsky asks:
"What could have brought, together in quick succession, all these animals and plants, from the tundra of the Arctic Circle and from the jungle of the tropics.... from lands of many latitudes and altitudes, from freshwater lakes and rivers, and from the salt seas of the north and south? The molluscs with closed valves furnish evidence that the molluscs did not die a natural death but were buried alive.

"It would appear that the agglomeration was brought together by a moving force that rushed overland, left in its wake marine sand and deep-water creatures, swept animals and trees from the south to the north, and then, turning from the polar regions back toward the warm regions, mixed its burden of arctic plants and animals in the same sediment where it had left those from the south. Animals and plants of land and sea from various parts of the world were thrown together, one group upon another, by some elemental force that could not have been an overflowing river."[9]

Joseph Prestwich, professor of geology at Oxford (1874-88), regarded as the foremost authority on the geology of the Ice Age in England, was compelled to admit that it was "impossible to account for the specific geological phenomena... by any agency of which our time has offered us experience."[10]

"The agency, whatever it was, must have acted with sufficient violence to smash the bones."[11]

"Nor could this have been the work of a long time, for the entombed bones, though much broken, are singularly fresh."[12]

Prestwich was compelled to admit that "the south of England had been submerged to the depth of not less than about 1,000 feet".[13]

Germany

Coal beds in Geiseltal contain a complete mixture of plants, insects and animals from all climatic zones of the world, in one

common grave. There are remains of apes, marsupials, crocodiles, American condor, giant tropical snakes, and salamanders. Some are from swamps, others from plains. **Their muscles and skin are perfectly preserved.**
There is an entire stratum of leaves from all parts of the earth.
Beautifully coloured tropical beetles retain the soft parts of the body; **even the contents of the intestines are preserved intact.**

Although leaves are preserved in fresh condition (retaining their fine fibre and green colour) and insects their membranes and **colours perfectly preserved**, ALL ARE VIOLENTLY TORN INTO PIECES.

It appears they were carried there by onrushing water – from all parts of the world???

Gibraltar

Numerous crevices down to 290 feet (29 stories) deep on the Rock of Gibraltar are filled with bones of the wolf, bear, lynx, hare, ibex, rabbit, horse, panther, rhinoceros, ox, wild boar, deer and other animals. The bones are neither worn, rolled, nor gnawed. They are splintered and broken. And found at that depth together with land and marine shells – as well as coral.[14]

Prestwich considers: "A great and common danger, such as a great flood, alone could have driven together the animals of the plains and of the crags and caves."[15]

A handful of bone samples still in the Natural History Museum in London confirm their "freshness", indicating that they had been entombed with the flesh still on them – and not eaten by predators.

Excavations of all other Gibraltar caves by men such as A. Craven Greenwood, J. Waechter, D.A.E. Garrod and R. Wilson testify to the bones' consistently unrolled and fresh appearance. Flood, not glacial, action is indicated.

These fissures are at different altitudes, the highest being at 1,100 feet.

Sicily

Huge piles of bones exist in the hills around Palermo. Bones of hippopotamus, deer, ox and elephant were mixed together in wild confusion, again without sign of weathering or gnawing. The fact that bones of animals **of all ages** were piled together, indicates that the catastrophe was SUDDEN.

Malta

On the island of Malta are caves crammed full of hares, lemurs, tigers, rhinoceros, elephants – **and birds**. **Giant swans** (twice as large as any swans now on earth) **and huge sea birds** are crammed in with the animals.

Now Malta is **an island** 170 miles (270 km) from the nearest other land (Sicily).

And please note, these birds are sea birds. Had this been a mere local flood, these giant swans would have taken off for Sicily and been there in half an hour.

These sea birds would never have been drowned – they're sea birds! So what happened? These birds **kept flying until they could fly no more**!!!

Another huge fissure yielded an abundant mixture of birds, sharks' teeth, fish bones, frogs, turtles and shells. With these were stones of various sizes which were strange to that locality – including 15-foot blocks of stone, grooved and hollowed by violent water action. Only water could have deposited and mixed these remains in the manner in which they are found.

Cyprus

Up Bufelvento, about 2,000 feet high, is a huge deposit of pygmy hippopotamus (these are a river-side animal).

Think about this. **What do you think lifted, crushed and mixed with sea shells** a huge herd of pygmy hippopotamus? **What swept the herd right up the mountain** to 2,000 feet above sea level, until it found a depression to deposit them? **And then rolled over the top of them**, and left them there?

What but a universal flood did that? A flood which rushed right over the top of Bufelvento, 2,000 feet above sea level, would, like or not, be capable of rolling over continents!

Greece

On the island of Cerigo, near Corfu, 135 different animals have been identified from a bone bed a mile in circumference.

Lebanon
The same mixture of **LAND** animals and **SEA** shells is found in caves and fissures near Beirut and elsewhere.

ALL OVER WESTERN EUROPE, IN RUSSIA, and in islands such as CORSICA and SARDINIA, **fissures** are choked with bones. The bones are **broken** into innumerable fragments. They are still "**fresh**". **Artifacts of man** are found among them. Fissures are in rocks **on top of isolated hills**. Often, **birds** and **animals** are MIXED TOGETHER WITH **trees** and vegetation. These all seem to have been washed into the fissures.

THE CAUSE
QUESTION: "COULD THEY HAVE FALLEN IN ALIVE, OR BEEN BURIED THERE?"
The answer is no, for there are no complete skeletons.
QUESTION: "COULD THEY HAVE BEEN BROUGHT THERE BY STREAMS?"
Again, no, for there are no signs of them having been rolled.
QUESTION: "COULD THEY HAVE BEEN SLAUGHTERED BY RUTHLESS MEN?"
No, there could have been no way to bury them in such numbers before other animals gnawed them or the weather affected them. Considering the number of the remains found, thrown together in great heaps, mixed in great confusion, large and small animals, grass-eating and flesh-eating animals and birds, all in one pile, buried in alluvial deposits, intermingled with remains of plants and trees, seashells and fish, such an idea becomes absurd.
QUESTION: "DID SOME DISEASE STRIKE THEM DOWN?"
All animals at the same time and in every part of the world? Land animals and deep sea creatures, all mixed together? Of course not.

Certainly animals stricken by sudden disease would be too weak to ascend to the hilltops!

The bones could not have been exposed to weather for long, for none of them shows marks of weathering.

That water deposited them is indicated by the very general cementing together of the bones by calcite.

Moreover, these bone-filled chasms are usually found on isolated hills of considerable height – places on which we might expect animals to gather in seeking safety from an approaching flood.

This scene is enacted on hundreds of thousands of hills in every part of the earth.

DEPTH OF FLOOD WATERS

QUESTION: "WAS THE WATER VERY DEEP OVER THE LAND?"

"According to Prestwich, the rubble deposit in England indicates that the country was **submerged to a depth of at least one thousand feet**, while on the Continent we find evidence of **submergence up to three thousand feet**."[16]

Water, as you know, pans out to its own level. If, as we are seeing, Flood waters raged across Europe and the Mediterranean at such a height, **could the rest of the world have escaped?**

Let's start travelling and take in some more localities. If you're not already amazed, you soon will be...

6
Fissures of Bones (b) -
THE SUDDENNESS

While panicked men, women and animals were rushing to the highest points in Europe, the very same scene was being enacted all over the world.
Let's turn our attention now to North America.

California
Found buried together in the San Pedro Valley, were the remains of **sharks, seals, porpoises, sea urchins, molluscs** – AND LAND VERTEBRATES (mammals and birds).[1]

Near Los Angeles are the La Brea Asphalt Pits, containing the bones of hundreds of animals and birds – sabre-toothed tigers, horses, camels, mammoths, mastodons, bison, peacocks, and so on – all apparently CAUGHT SUDDENLY. They are "broken, mashed, contorted, and mixed in a most heterogeneous mass, such as could never have resulted from the chance trapping and burial of a few stragglers."[2] With those animals were the bones of one human.

Velikovsky asks: "Could it be that at this particular spot large herds of wild beasts, mostly carnivorous, were overwhelmed by falling gravel, tempests, tides and raining bitumen?"[3]

Maryland
Cumberland Cave is a closed fissure containing fossils from different climatic zones and different habitats, mixed in one great mass. The bones of southern tropical animals (tapir, crocodilid and peccary) are jumbled together with northern animals (mink, elk, lemming, wolverine, hare, muskrat, shrew, red squirrel, porcupine and others). Animals that now live in arid regions are heaped together with animals from areas of plentiful water supply. Woodland creatures are intermingled with those of the open terrain.

J.W. Gidley notes: "This strange assemblage of fossil remains occurs hopelessly intermingled..."[4]

Death overtook them all at the same time. As the bones are very broken yet showing no sign of being water worn, it appears that the animals were dashed against rocks and their bones broken inside their bodies by that water avalanche that smashed them all together. After this, rocks and gravel sealed them in.

Utah and Colorado

In Dinosaur National Monument (covering parts of Utah and Colorado), jumbled remains show signs of tumbling and washing about by water.

Wyoming

In Lincoln County, deposits include fish, mollusca, crustaceans, alligators, turtles, birds, mammals, insects and plants, including palm leaves 6 to 8 feet in length. So many of these specimens are so **perfectly preserved** they had to be piled together and entombed SUDDENLY.

Human remains have been found in a number of North American caves. For example, Conkling or Bishop's Cap Cave in the Organ Mountains, New Mexico.

Scattered human bones were deposited chaotically with those of camel, horse, bison, antelope, rodents, wolf, ground-sloth, coyote, and other animals.

Canada

Concerning fossil beds along the Red Deer River, Dr. Allen, professor of geology at the University of Alberta, made the observation that they "seem to have been driven together by a common danger and to have perished in the same great catastrophe."[5]

South America

A whole field of mastodon bones lies near Bogota, Colombia. Their sudden, simultaneous destruction is indicated by the quantity of bones found at one spot.

A number of caves investigated around Lagoa to Sumidouro, near Santa Lucia, by Lund, contained bones of humans. These were mingled with those of jaguars, horses and other animals.[6]

In one cave were the remains of over 50 humans of every age from infant to old man. They were mixed together in confusion with animals. Both human and animal remains possessed the same chemical composition. This indicates they were contemporaneous.[7]

In mountain fissures of the South American continent, multitudes of animals continue to be discovered.

D'Orbigny, Darwin's successor, had the courage to admit:

"I argue that this destruction was caused by an invasion of the continent by water... the Pampas mud was deposited suddenly as the result of violent floods of water.... Even in places 200 leagues apart..."[8]

Australia

"Evidence clearly echoing all this has come to light in various Australian caves. Ice-sheets like those advocated by orthodox glaciologists were, of course, conspicuously **absent from Australia**, so this evidence is especially significant. It occurs, for example: ...in caverns... at Wellington; at Boree; near the head of the Colo river; at Yesseba, on the Macleay river; at the head of the Coodradigbee; not far from the head of the Bogan, and in other places."[9]

Concerning the Wellington Valley bones, Lang noted:

"Frequently these occur so fixed between large rocks that it is quite impossible to get them out; and indeed, in general, none can be got in an entire state from the matrix, being in their embedded state full of fractures; ...the bones were in... abundance, and generally upright... the animals that owned these bones could not have died a natural death, for most of them have evidently been subjected to great violence, and exhibit fractures in every direction."[10]

Another observer wrote:

"Heads, jaw-bones, teeth, ribs, and femurs are all jumbled and concreted together without reference to parts... if the bones had been so separated and dispersed and broken into minute fragments, as they now appear in this breccia, while they were still bound together by ligaments, it is difficult to imagine how that could take place under any natural process with which we are acquainted... the best specimens of single bones have been found wedged between huge rocks, where the breccia is found like mortar between them, in situations eight or ten fathoms underground."[11]

In bone caves at Coodradigbee, remains were found over 200 feet (61.5 metres) below ground level.[12]

In Australian caves, it is precisely the same scenario as in Europe, Asia, and elsewhere – namely, countless assorted animals (including some apparently dismembered while still in the flesh) entombed chaotically and violently and crowded unnaturally into small rock cavities and crevices.

Africa

In a 1947 issue of the Illustrated London News, Dr. Brown, the South African fossil logist, and a vigorous evolutionist, spoke of the Kara fossil formation around Johannesburg. He acknowledged that over 200,000 square miles there are, just under the surface, **the complete skeletons of 800 billion individuals** (mostly amphibians or reptiles), **all killed at the same time** (since they are all in the same formation). This multitude of animals were **all buried at the same time.**

Now, here is my question. Let's be fair about this.

What – but a universal flood – killed and **buried** simultaneously 800 billion individuals?

Nothing buries animals like **water**.

Ice does **not** bury animals. You wouldn't expect it to. Animals have sense. Glaciers travel only a few feet per year.

Siberia

During the late 1700s, P.S. Pallis visited large areas of Siberia. In the Irtish River valley, he found bones of mammoths and other extinct animals, and nearby the heads of great fishes. **Land mammoths and sea fish**. And elsewhere a petrified jawbone, coated with sea mussels.[13]

He regarded these as having "...come from a great inundation."[14]

A **whale** skeleton was found far inland in the Chukchee peninsula of north eastern Siberia. This whale was still partially covered by skin, with deep red, almost fresh flesh adhering to many of its bones.

River floods had partly eroded the frozen sand enveloping it the preceding winter. Because exposure of the carcass to even one summer's sun would have induced putrefaction long ago, there could be no doubt of the specimen's very great antiquity.

It was found at the same level as bones of **mammoths and other animals**.[15]

Ocean whales – what could mix them up with tropical land animals?

Again, a **mammoth** was found at Troitzkoe near Moscow in 1846, associated with plant fragments, **fish scales and bones** and pieces of cod.[16]

India

From Kashmir through to China the cataclysm uprooted trees and threw sand over animals **in mountains thousands of feet high**.

The Siwulik Hills, north of Delhi, are 2,000 to 3,000 feet high. Hippopotamus, ape, pig, rhinoceros, tortoise, elephant and ox fill the interior of the hills to bursting.

China

Rock fissures in Chou Kou Tien, near Beijing, contained bones of animals from all climatic areas of the world (cool, tropical, dry and wet), "in a strange mixture," and the fractured bones of seven humans, all embedded in a mixture of clay and sand.[17]

Korea

China and Korea are riddled with fissures and caverns closely packed with animal remains and sea shells. Again, amazingly "fresh".

Burma

Central Burma has deposits 10,000 feet deep! Two great horizontal masses of fossils are separated by a 4,000 foot depth of water-laid sands. The deposits also contain huge quantities of fossil wood. Hundreds of thousands of entire trunks suggest the destruction of thick forests.[18]

Velikovsky comments:

"Animals met death and extinction by the elementary forces of nature, which also uprooted forests and from Kashmir to Indo-China **threw sand over species and genera in mountains thousands of feet high**."[19]

Similar finds of animal graveyards, mixed with human artefacts, have been unearthed ALL OVER ASIA.

ONLY A FLOOD COULD DO IT

It is clear that nothing but a flood would have driven such strange mixtures of animals – animals that don't normally live together – into caves and crevices in all parts of the world. And buried them together.

The evidence everywhere strongly suggests that they were drowned **en masse** by violent water action. This bone-cave phenomenon is **of world-wide extent**.

Was this a global Flood? Of course it was.

And apart from the burials in caves and crevices, we have noted **vast fossil graveyards** in sedimentary (water-laid) rock. These average **a mile deep**, around the globe.

RAPID BURIAL

The very existence of fossils indicates two basic facts:
1. rapid burial of the organism
2. followed by rapid compaction of the sediments encasing them.

Otherwise they would not have been preserved.

Here is a fact of utmost importance: ANIMALS OF EVERY KIND DIED IN GREAT NUMBERS AND WERE BURIED ALMOST INSTANTLY.

Each of these animals, by the unbelievable uniformitarian explanation, fell into their graveyards by accident – one at a time!

However, the facts reveal not normal, slow processes, but unusual transportation and rapid burial mechanisms.

THOUSANDS of feet of depth of such fossils (to a worldwide average of one mile deep) required **rapid burial under great pressure**.

Many times the remains of animals are **pressed flat** by the huge weight of the sediment layers above them. These creatures are found **crushed**, EVEN TO THE CELLULAR STRUCTURE!

This could only have occurred if the strata which contained them HAD NOT HARDENED before the next layers above were deposited. The weight of these higher layers piling up **compressed the strata**

below, which was still fresh and soft, and crushed the still-soft bodies it contained.

This proves RAPID DEPOSITION of large volumes of sediments in quick succession. I shall repeat it: there was no time for hardening first.

I would hate to be an evolutionist trying to explain this. Present-day processes are NOT a key to the past. As Whitcomb and Morris observe:

"To attempt to account for these vast graveyards in terms of present-day processes and events, except via the most extreme and unscientific extrapolation, is absolutely impossible! And yet it is in deposits such as these that **most** of the fossils are found on which is based much of the generally accepted uniformitarian scheme of historical geology."[20]

Then there are petrified animals. Such creatures had first to be rapidly buried. They had to be entirely under ground, so that minerals and water could work on them before they decomposed. The noted evolutionist, L.S.B. Leakey, writing of caterpillars, a beetle and soft insects perfectly turned to stone, asks: "How did these incredible fossils occur? We simply do not know."[21]

DINOSAURS LIKEWISE DROWNED

Yes, big as they were, dinosaurs suffered the same watery fate – followed by rapid burial. This is evidence that some scientists prefer to ignore.

Great dinosaur beds have been excavated in Alberta, Belgium, New Mexico, Tanzania, Spitzbergen and many other places.

All over the world, paleontologists have found caches of fossilized dinosaurs that were buried instantly in a catastrophic movement of water.[22]

In 1877, 20 complete skeletons of the giant Iguanadon were found in the rocks of a Belgian coal mine at Bernissant. The rocks themselves show they were buried in a raging flood of water and mud. These Iguanadon are now on display at the Royal Museum of Natural History in Brussels.

In the Gobi desert a large predatory dinosaur was found still clutching the skull of its victim – a small armoured dinosaur. Some reptiles are found with their skeletons curled up in a sleeplike posture;

others in walking, standing and paddling positions. The animals were caught and buried as they went about their various activities. Others were killed as they struggled to escape. They were preserved in large numbers.

A gliding pterosaur enclosed the skeletons of two fish species in its pouch.

The stomachs of ichthyosaurs (dolphin-shaped sea reptiles) also contain remains of prey. Others were giving birth as burial suddenly came to them (see picture below).

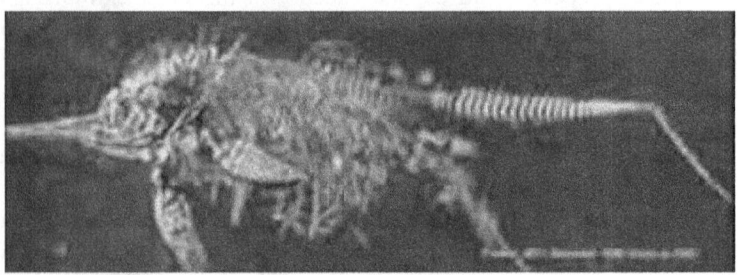

"Many entire skeletons of duck-billed dinosaurs have been excavated in... a swimming position with the head thrown back as if in death throes."[23] It seems that in their death throes they were STRAINING TO KEEP THEIR HEADS ABOVE WATER!

At Dinosaur National monument, which lies partly in Utah and partly in Colorado, none of the dinosaur skeletons are complete. The bones lie as if they had been tumbled together. They are probably lying as they were washed together by the waters of the Great Flood.

Evolutionists have had to devise elaborate theories to explain why these animals, which are **not aquatic**, should have died violently in water.

Their contorted shapes, their massive numbers in fossil graveyards, as well as the presence of whole skeletons showing evidence of rapid burial, all speak of a colossal flood.

These mass entombments are what would be expected if there indeed occurred something like the biblical Flood in ancient times. This is particularly likely in light of the fact that these water-borne graveyards appear all over the planet.

*Dinosaur footprints in sandstone that shows water ripples
(Photo: H.G.Coffin)*

Joe Taylor of Mt. Blanco Fossil Museum in Texas announced in 2003:

"At our T-rex site this summer in Montana, we found with the Rex, parts of a Triceratops, Hadrosaur and Raptor (all land animals) mixed with crocodile teeth, closed clams and turtles (probably water turtles). In the Colorado Morrison formation site, we found Sauropods, Stegosaur and Allosaur (also land animals) mixed with fish, crocodile and turtles. One big Sauropod is upside down, and an Ankylosaur 10 feet away is also probably upside down. As far as I know all Ankylosaurs found to date in the USA are buried upside down, indicating water burial."[24]

Dinosaurs and men both perished in The Deluge

It is important to note that there is much evidence that dinosaurs and men did live side by side. We shall uncover a little of this evidence in Chapters 13 and 18.

There was **mass extinction** in all parts of the world simultaneously – and **sudden burial**! WHAT WOULD IT TAKE TO DO THIS?

Creatures long dead speak with thundertones to this generation; not of slow evolutionary development and burial, but of a violent global Flood.

* * * * * * *

And had this not occurred, Nikita Borshev might never have enjoyed his Moscow banquet.

Let's drop in on him.

FISSURES OF BONES – Summary

WHY FOSSILS ARE SOMETIMES IN ASCENDING ORDER

First the lowest creatures inhabiting the deep ocean were overwhelmed and buried. The waters and disturbed sediments then overtook the amphibians and the land-bordering creatures. As the Flood waters advanced, the swamp, marsh and river-flat creatures were overtaken, including reptiles.

Most land animals and humans, with their greater mobility, were able to escape temporarily to higher ground as the waters rose.

The general order of buried fossils (from "simple" on the bottom to "complex" on top) is thus exactly what would be expected in such a catastrophe.

HOW FLOOD WATERS OVERTOOK THE ASCENDING ANIMALS

Gripped by the same terror, wild beasts and tame stampeded to higher ground. In great numbers they thronged together – until the waters rose and covered them. Then the huge waves smashed upon them large rocks and debris, until their bones were crushed or smashed. So the bones of the large and small, the gentle and ferocious, were thrown together in wild confusion in a common grave.

ANIMAL GRAVEYARDS

All over the world, the cataclysm uprooted trees and threw sand and rocks over animals which had gathered on mountains. Thousands of feet up, many were washed into crevices and held tight.

On every continent, and in numerous places, are vast "fossil graveyards", where masses of creatures have been swept to a sudden death in their millions. These areas are packed with land and sea creatures from different habitats and even from different climatic regions – all **mixed and buried together in a completely unnatural way**.

For months longer, the storm raged. Unceasingly, in repeating 12 hour cycles, the mighty ebb and flow wore down the earth's surface and each wave returned with its debris. Travelling long distances under water, fast moving currents of suspended mud and sand spread out over thousands of square miles. The ebb and flow laid down successive strata, alternately burying land organisms and water creatures, to ultimately fossilise. As well as laying down strata, the Flood sorted debris into piles here and there.

THESE FOSSIL GRAVEYARDS SPEAK NOT OF SLOW EVOLUTIONARY DEVELOPMENT AND BURIAL, BUT OF A VIOLENT GLOBAL FLOOD.

7

Frozen graveyards -
INTERRUPTED DINNER

Nikita Borshev fiddled with his tie. His wife came to assist him. He was chuckling. "Natasha, my dear, it's going to be some mother of a night!"

Couldn't contain himself now. Yes, I'll tell her, he decided. "Heh, heh, Tasha," he laughed. "Are they in for a shock! They'll never know what hit them!"

His mirth was now uncontrollable. His body was shaking.

"Keep still," she scolded. "Or you'll have to do your own tie. Whatever's got you tonight?"

He was still roaring. It really had the better of him now. "Heh, Tasha, it's a scream. Do you know, they'll think they're eating steak. But we're going to serve them MAMMOTH! Get it? Dead mammoth flesh. And it's all of 4,000 years old!"

... Nikita and, indeed, his fellow scientists, had an unforgettable banquet that night.

Not that they were the first. Early this century, in the dreary frozen waste of northern Siberia, where neither tree nor shrub will grow, a hunter saw his dogs tearing into an object protruding from the ice. On investigation, he discovered it to be a perfectly-preserved tropical mammoth, a type of large elephant.

The refrigeration has been so perfect that mammoth carcasses – snap-frozen long ago – have been thawed to feed dogs.

And that's not all...

THE MYSTERY OF THE "MUCK"

Frozen soil constitutes one of the greatest mysteries on our planet. It covers 1/7 of the earth's land surface.

This frozen "muck", as it is called, is composed of an assortment of sand, earth, bones and decaying vegetable and animal remains – all bound together with frozen water, which acts virtually as a rock.

It spreads across northern Asia, Alaska and the top of Canada.

When it thaws, it becomes a soup, often with an appalling stench, from the masses of preserved, semi-decayed or fully decayed matter.

In some places, drilling has proceeded down through it to over 4,000 feet, but still without reaching solid rock.

Today this region is up to 65 degrees BELOW zero, swept by icy winds. It is naked Tundra, in which virtually nothing will grow.

ALASKA

Bulldozers over a wide area near Fairbanks have been scraping this UNNATURAL MIXTURE into flumes to wash out the gold particles scattered through it all.

The list of animals thawed out of it would fill several pages. There are mammoths, rhinoceroses, horses, giant oxen, huge tigers, giant bison, wolves, beavers, lions, musk ox, ground squirrel, sheep and species now extinct – as well as plants which grow only in a warm climate.

Oil drillers in Northern Alaska brought up an 18 inch long chunk of tree trunk from almost 1,000 feet below the surface. It wasn't petrified – just frozen.

Perfectly preserved

In some areas, eyes, trunks, feet and delicate tissues of animals are perfectly preserved, as are undigested fir and pine inside their stomachs.

North of Fairbanks, in the Yukon Valley, the deep frozen **stomachs** of woolly mammoths were found to contain leaves and grass. **Babies lay beside their mothers.**

Clay and earth were laid over them, then it SUDDENLY FROZE.

Professor Frank Hibben, an archaeologist from the University of New Mexico, concluded that 'THE WHOLE WORLD OF ANIMALS AND PLANTS WAS SUDDENLY FROZEN IN MID-MOTION.'[1]

Unparalleled violence

There is also evidence of unparalleled violence. Hibben describes it:

"Mammoth and bison alike were torn and twisted as though by a cosmic hand in godly rage. In one place we can find the foreleg and shoulder of a mammoth with portions of the flesh and the toenails and the hair still clinging to the blackened bones. Close by is the neck and skull of a bison with the vertebrae clinging together with tendons and ligaments and the chitinous covering of the horns intact. There is no mark of a knife or cutting instrument. The animals were simply torn apart and scattered over the landscape like things of straw and string, even though some of them weighed several tons. **Mixed with** the piles of bones are trees, also twisted and torn and piled in tangled groups; **and the whole is covered** with the fine sifting muck, then frozen solid."[2]

What was it that swept the entire tangled mass of trees and animals and piled them in great heaps over thousands of square miles?

Layers of volcanic ash are interspersed through the piles of bones and tusks.

There is an interesting statement in the book of Genesis that toward the close of the Flood "God made a **great wind** to pass over the earth."[3]

One can imagine that, as the Flood waters abated, these remains lay scattered over the ground. The fury of the wind tore them apart, mixing them with the Flood debris. A suddenly lowered temperature then froze the muck before the bodies could decompose much further.

SIBERIA

In Siberia today, winters last for ten months. Summer does not begin until July, and winter resumes during early August. Then come terribly icy winds – and in January the cold registers 65 degrees below zero. On the dreary, frozen waste of northern Siberia, neither tree nor shrub will grow.

Yet under the ground lie huge hoards of tropical and temperate animals, whose appetites once needed corresponding supplies of food.

The whole of Siberia is one vast graveyard!

Bones of elephants are interspersed with those of frozen sheep, frozen horses, frozen camels, antelopes, bison, huge felines, oxen, rhinos and other tropical animals. And these are in numbers which defy all calculation.

Wedged so close together, they form hills on land and underwater ledges on islands. In fact, they occur everywhere: on river banks, plains, on rising ground and in frozen cliffs.

A tantalising mystery are the countless mammoths found in frozen earth or muck. What really caused all this muck – silt, sand, pebbles and boulders – with all the junk that is found in it, EVEN DOWN TO THOUSANDS OF FEET?

The Siberian mammoths, twice the weight of today's largest elephants, stood 15 feet high, with tusks up to 10 feet long; and the tusks weighed 180 to 200 pounds (almost 100 kilograms). The tusks of today's African elephant weigh only 40 to 50 pounds.

These quick-frozen mammoths have for thousands of years produced "fresh" ivory for Chinese carvings. In just twenty years (from 1880 to 1900), about 20,000 pairs of beautiful ivory tusks were taken from just one "mine" in Siberia. More than half the world's supply of ivory, many piano keys and billiard balls, have come from these tusks.

It is estimated that no less than 7 million mammoths must have perished in Siberia, along with multitudes of other animals.

"The mammoth and mastodon seem at one time to have been common over the whole surface of the globe... The Siberian deposits... appear to be as inexhaustible as a coalfield."[4]

It is beyond comprehension how any region could supply food for so many monstrous creatures, as well as so many other animals.

Of course, this very fact offers INCONTESTABLE PROOF of the grandeur of the world which perished in the Great Flood.

Mammoths are often found in hills of frozen driftwood, called by local people "*Noah's wood*".

Frozen display "windows"

On the shores of the Arctic Ocean are banks of ice, split with deep chasms. Peering into their depths, one sees at the bottom masses of tusks, bones and skulls.

Cliffs behind the beaches are packed with bones. In summer, portions thaw and crash to the beach below. To a beach walker, the spectacle is unforgettable – icebergs stranded on the beach, together with long distances of tropical mammoth remains – tusks, teeth and bones.

Sometimes, COMPLETE BODIES WITH FLESH, FUR AND HAIR PERFECT, can be seen standing in the frozen cliffs!

Inland for enormous distances into the vast interior of the continent, the **whole** ground seems often to be formed of masses of bones welded together.

Without exception, every river that cuts its way through the plain has exposed the strata, to reveal quadrupeds entombed in enormous quantities. The bottoms and sides of rivers are loaded with bones, teeth and tusks of animals.

The sea off the coast is shallow. Whenever there is a storm, fresh supplies of bones are left exposed on the mud banks in the middle of the sea. (Of course, this shows that the strata forming the bottom of the sea are likewise full of fossils.)

"Islands of bones"
Some islands or high points where the animals went for refuge seem to be made entirely of their bones.

On the New Siberian Islands, bones of 66 animal species, along with enormous petrified forests of tree trunks are heaped hundreds of feet high in wild disorder, broken and charred.

There are found shells from a warmer climate, and whole trees, such as plum trees, **with their leaves and fruit**. (No such trees grow within 2,000 miles, today.)

Llakov Island, Kotaini Island (over 100 miles long) and **many other islands ARE ACTUALLY COMPOSED OF COUNTLESS SKELETONS**, cemented together by icy sand. The bones are "fresh." On the shores, tusks stick up like tree trunks in the frozen sand.

Hundreds of miles further east are the Bear Islands. Here the same condition of abundant fossil remains is seen. According to Ferdinand Petrovitch von Wrangel, a Russian explorer, these fossil remains "seem to form the chief substance of the islands."[5]

Perfectly preserved
Sometimes complete carcasses have been recovered. Mammoths have been found with their **eyeballs still in place, plant food in their stomachs** and **half-chewed grasses on their tongues**!

One was found after its head became exposed during a landslide. In its mouth was half-chewed food, but **its bones had been suddenly broken**.

Another **died so suddenly**, it was still chewing grasses and flowers; in its stomach were buttercups and flowering wild beans. Its legs were broken. It had been knocked to its knees, then frozen, and had remained frozen ever since.

In the mouths of others were bluebells, sedges and grasses; or willow, maple and cedar leaves, their last meal. THEY DID NOT HAVE TIME TO SWALLOW.

One was found with unchewed bean pods, still containing the beans, still between its teeth. The stomach of another contained 24 pounds of undigested vegetable matter. The color of the leaves of one plant was still intact, as if freshly picked.

A mammoth unearthed in 1908 was found lying on some green grass, frozen with the carcass.

The skin of the preserved mammoths is congested with red blood corpuscles. This proves **death was due to suffocation by gases or drowning** – despite the fact that the elephant is a very long and strong swimmer.

Small ice crystals are found in the blood, indicating that they probably froze in less than five hours. If they had frozen slowly, the crystals would be bigger.

They were literally frozen alive, before decomposition could occur – either to them, or to the food in their stomachs.

"Mummies" served at a banquet

After 4,300 years, the flesh of these giant mummies is in such instant frozen condition, so well preserved, that sledge dogs and men have eaten it without ill effects.

According to the Russian journal *Isvestia* and the U.S.S.R. Academy of Science, steaks from a mammoth were served to scientists at a banquet in Moscow. Harles Berlitz relates that prior to the banquet, "the scientists did not know what they were to be served but, according to reports, they found the meat moderately palatable."[6]

In 1972, at an Explorer's Club banquet in New York City, flesh from a horse found frozen in the Alaska permafrost was served on toast as an **hors d'oeuvre** – and the explorers went back for "seconds".

HOW DID THEY DIE?

THEORY ONE: They died from freak accidents. They fell onto the ice (one by one).

Answer: Except for the upper slopes of some mountains, there have never been glaciers in Siberia. Furthermore, no animals have been found in ice – but always in the muck **This indicates that water engulfed them.**

Certainly these animals did **not** die from freak accidents, as is often suggested. This is obvious from the great number of bones interred with them in the same strata – bones of millions of mammoths alone, as well as of numerous other types of animals.

THEORY TWO: They fell into rivers and were then washed into estuaries and deltas and covered in silt.

Answer: The remains are not in estuaries, deltas or swamps. They are scattered all over the country. Most are not along the low coast. Almost all of them are embedded in the **highest** levels of the low plateaus all over the tundra. Surely all of northern Asia, Canada and Alaska could never have been one vast delta, nor could rivers have wandered all over this higher land, depositing muck uphill. And bear in mind that many of these animals were found undamaged, fresh and standing and kneeling upright – none of which would be the case if they had been carried by rivers.

THEORY THREE: Because they are animals of the tropics, they must have been swept by rivers, from warmer southern lands, northward to the arctic.

Answer:
1. They are found in territories where there are no rivers.
2. They are found more often in elevations near higher hills than along the low coast or on the flat tundra.
3. Mammoth remains are also found on rivers that flow SOUTH, such as the Ural and the Volga, rivers which could not have carried carcasses northward.
4. Many carcasses have been found in a standing, upright position inconceivable in a floating carcass.

ONE SUDDEN EVENT

Everywhere the animals are in their prime, apparently in robust health. They were entombed before they had a chance to decay. Their bones are ungnawed by carnivores, who instead, were buried with them.

The geologist J.D. Dana notes: "It is evident that these animals were feeding in a tropical climate when the sudden crisis came and the summer climate abruptly ended and became **suddenly** extreme as of a single winter's night, never again relenting."[7]

George McCready Price relates: "But suddenly an awful change took place. The exact details of how it occurred may still be somewhat uncertain; but that it was **astonishingly sudden**, and that it must have been a change **affecting the entire world**, seems as certain as man's own existence. As a well-known geologist remarks, this genial climate in which these animals lived was '**abruptly terminated**...'"[8]

"This sudden and world-wide change of climate is somehow intimately connected with geological exchange of land and water and the formation of we know not how much of the geological deposits, and serves to mark, in the words of Howorth, the 'great dividing line' between that old world, with its perpetual summer, and our present world, with its terrific extremes of heat and cold.... That this change occurred within the human epoch is conceded by every scientist."[9]

Harold T. Wilkins observes thus: "Signs of thick sediments around show that a great and widespread flood came roaring on them...."[10]

Of course, these animals did not have to float around on the Arctic Ocean for months. They were quickly buried. As Whitcomb and Morris express it: "The entrapped waters in these sediments, cut off from the warm waters of the open ocean, froze rapidly, forming the 'permafrost,' the permanently frozen soils and subsoils of the Arctic lands."[11]

Although complete carcasses and skeletons are sometimes found, the remains usually look as if they had been torn about by some gigantic force.

Charles Darwin, who denied the occurrence of past catastrophe, admitted that this phenomenon was for him an insoluble problem.

The English scientist Sir Henry Howarth comments:

"Now by no physical process known to us can we understand how soft flesh could thus be buried in ground while it is frozen as hard as flint without disintegrating it. We cannot push an elephant's body into a mass of solid ice or hard frozen gravel without entirely destroying the fine articulations and pounding the whole mass into a jelly.... When we, therefore, meet with great carcasses of mammoths with their most delicate tissues, their eyes, trunks and feet beautifully preserved and lying several feet underground in hard frozen, undisturbed gravel and clay, we cannot escape the conclusion that when these carcasses were buried, the ground was soft and yielding. The facts compel us to admit that when the mammoth was buried in Siberia, the ground was soft and the climate therefore comparatively mild and genial, that immediately afterwards, the same ground became frozen, and the same climate became arctic, and that they have remained so to this day, and this was not gradually and in accordance with some slowly continuous, astronomical, or cosmical changes, but suddenly and 'per saltum.'"[12]

Instances of preservation extend over the length of the continent. They are preserved in the same perfect way, showing evidence of a sudden climatic change. We can only conclude that they all bear witness to **A COMMON EVENT**.

WHAT CAUSED THIS INSTANT FREEZE?

Henry Hiebert suggests:

"An extremely interesting side effect of such a total precipitation of all the moisture in such a vapour canopy, and perhaps all the carbon dioxide in the atmosphere as well, would be **a sudden and extreme lowering of the temperature on a temporary basis**, i.e., long enough to quick freeze the vast herds of mammoths that had been trapped and buried in the Deluge mud and are now found by the hundreds of thousands in the Arctic permafrost. When a hydrological balance had been restored in the atmosphere, the temperatures could have improved to their present state."[13]

Ivan Sanderson explains further:

"...frozen-food experts have pointed out that to do this [quick-freeze], starting with a healthy, live specimen, you would have to drop the temperature of the air surrounding it down to a point well below minus 150 degrees Fahrenheit. There are two ways of freezing rapidly – one is by the blast method, the other by the mist process; these terms explain themselves. Moreover the colder air or any other gas becomes, the heavier it gets (Let's consider, for a moment, the intense volcanism at this time.) If these volcanic gases went up far enough they would be violently chilled and then, as they spiralled toward the poles, as all the atmosphere in time does, they would begin to descend. When they came upon a warm layer of air, they would weigh down upon it and pull all the heat out of it and then would eventually fall through it, probably with increasing momentum and perhaps in great blobs, pouring down through the weakest spot. And if they did this, the blob would displace the air already there, outward in all directions and with the utmost violence. Such descending gases might well be cold enough to kill and then instantly freeze a mammoth."[14]

It is possible that animals caught near the centre descending "blobs" of cold air before the winds began were enveloped in terrible cold, snap-frozen whole, non-violently.

Those just outside the area where the "blob" descended, were caught in exploding winds that literally tore them to bits, shredded them, then froze the whole lot.

Elsewhere, they were mangled, but had time to decompose before freezing. Still others were in areas where they decomposed down to bones; they were then either frozen, or not.

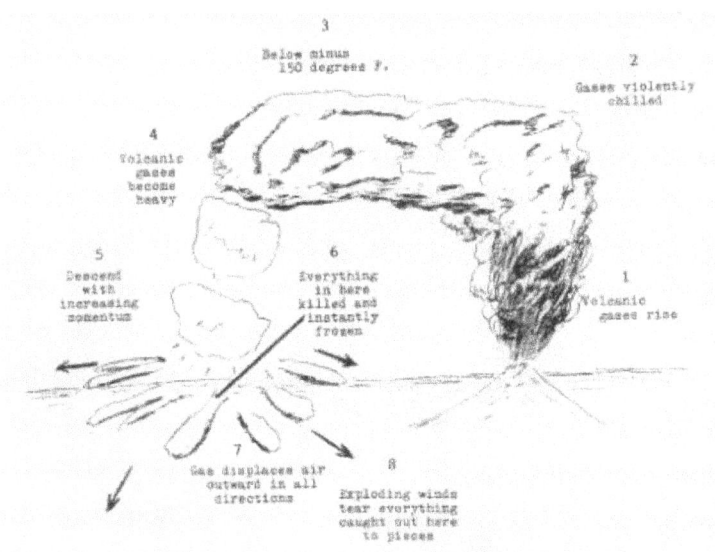

**How do you freeze
an elephant in 5 hours?**

Dr Kent Hovind suggests that a passing ice comet could have done this better.

He asks, "How do you freeze an elephant IN FIVE HOURS?"[15]

Then he asserts out that to freeze such enormous animals in less than five hours, you would need to place it in something at least 300 degrees Fahrenheit below zero.

However, nothing on earth could do it. It's a fact that it never gets 300 degrees below zero here on earth. According to *National Geographic* magazine, the coldest temperature ever recorded is 127 degrees below zero.

That's pretty chilly – but not cold enough to freeze the mammoths in 300 degrees below zero.

There are plenty of comets flying around and they are extremely cold – 300 to 400 degrees below zero. So there ARE super-cold objects in outer space. And these are cold enough to kill a mammoth and freeze it in five hours or less.

NO PRESENT EARTH PROCESS COULD DO IT

There is no natural process operating today that could possibly freeze such tons of flesh in the short time required to leave the mammoths in the quick-frozen condition in which they are found.

We see from these remains that:
1. An enormous catastrophe occurred.
2. This disaster involved a widespread flood of waters which buried them under continuous beds of gravel or loam.
3. The same catastrophe was accompanied by an intense, sudden change of climate.

While you're thinking about that, why not ponder these four questions:

SOMETHING TO ANSWER
1. What could kill animals, yet not break their bodies to pieces or even mutilate them?
2. What could disintegrate skeletons, without weathering the bones?
3. What could take up clay and gravel and cover the bodies with it?

4. What could sweep together animals of different species and sizes and mix them with trees and other vegetable debris?
Only one agent is capable of doing ALL THIS on a scale commensurate with the effects we see here in Siberia.
THAT AGENT IS **WATER.**

* * * * * * *

But now, let's go down to sun-drenched California, for the most "impossible" discovery you can ever imagine.

FROZEN GRAVEYARDS - Summary

ALASKA AND NORTHERN CANADA

The frozen soil of Alaska holds the remains of vegetation and animals "suddenly frozen in mid-motion." In some areas, eyes, trunks, feet and delicate tissues are perfectly preserved, as are the contents of food in their stomachs. Elsewhere, they are torn limb from limb as by a titanic force.

What was it that swept the entire tangled mass of trees and animals and piled them in great heaps over thousands of square miles – then suddenly froze them?

SIBERIA

The whole of Siberia is one vast graveyard of tropical and temperate animals. Some islands and hills where the animals apparently went for refuge seem to be made entirely of their bones. Elsewhere, the remains are frozen, together with other debris, thousands of feet deep.

At times, complete carcasses have been recovered. Mammoths have been found with their eyeballs still in place, plant food in their stomachs and half-chewed grasses on their tongues.

Instances of preservation extend over the length of the continent. They are preserved in the same perfect way, showing evidence of a sudden climatic change. We can only conclude that they all bear witness to a common event.

ONE SUDDEN EVENT

Everywhere the animals were in their prime, apparently in robust health. In water-borne sediment, they were entombed before they had a chance to decay, their bones ungnawed by carnivores, who instead, were buried with them.

They died so suddenly, they did not have time to swallow. They were snap frozen, before decomposition could occur.

ONLY WATER COULD DO IT

What could kill animals, yet not break their bodies to pieces or even mutilate them?

What same force could disintegrate skeletons, without weathering the bones? What could take up clay and gravel and cover the bodies with it? What could sweep together animals of different species and sizes and mix them with trees and other vegetable debris?

ONLY ONE AGENT IS CAPABLE OF DOING ALL THIS ON A CONTINENTAL SCALE. THAT AGENT IS WATER.

8

Sea-life cemeteries -

THE SECRET OF LOMPOC QUARRY

The quarry at Lompoc concealed a deathly secret.

Lompoc's 26,167 people had experienced several mild shocks over the years. But nothing like the bizarre surprise that now awaited them.

This sunny corner of southern California was noted for its production of garden-flower seeds. Its fruit and vegetable packing factories and its oil wells furnished a good income for some of its citizens. But there was something else, something very different, for which this town was famed. It produced earth products, mined and processed from the dead bodies of myriads of diatoms – microscopic sea creatures from long ago.

Now all eyes (perhaps that's overstating it) were on the diatom quarry. Slowly, even tediously, I suppose, workmen were uncovering something so big, so "unreal", it would nudge Lompoc into the evening news.

Just what this was, we shall discover shortly.

THE EXPERIMENT

Something very surprising was also about to occur across the continent, in Louisiana.

Have you ever wondered about that strange process that prevents a man or a tree, or for that matter a fish, from decaying, and instead turns it into a fossil? Or is that a subject as boring to you as dry bones?

We'll call this the Louisiana experiment.

Over in Louisiana, you see, a fascinating test had begun. The scientists were Rainer Zangerl and Eugenes Richardson. They would attempt to simulate the rapid burial process that seems to have been involved in the preservation of the fossils. If that were not feasible, they hoped at least to discover what natural method was responsible for the instant preservation.

Dead fish in wire cages were lowered into the black muds of several Louisiana lagoons and bayous.

Returning just 6½ days later, the scientists were shocked to find that all the soft parts of the fish were already reduced and all the bones scattered.

* * * * * * *

A marine scientist correctly states: "The life of most animals in the sea is terminated by their capture by other animals; those that die in other ways are sooner or later eaten by scavengers."[1]

Indeed, a dead fish is usually devoured in a matter of hours. In normal life, a dead fish's fins droop and colour fades. Even if transported by water a short distance, skeletons disintegrate.

FISH: SUDDEN DEATH

However, fossil fish are in COUNTLESS MILLIONS OF CASES found **in a marvellous state of preservation**, entombed over areas of tens of thousands of square miles, with all bones intact and every fin erect and intact; some even retain their colouring. Entire shoals of fish "are found in a state of agony, but with no mark of a scavenger's attack."[2]

These remains testify to MASS BURIAL WITHIN HOURS – not days – of death, before oxygen or bacteria could act upon them.

THROUGHOUT THE GLOBE, billions of fish show indications of violent death.

The ONLY AGENCY that could account for this is a SUDDEN convulsive and overpowering FLOOD of water-borne sediment.

North America
* Perfectly preserved fish extend from Siberia to the U.S.A. for 2,500 miles – with every scale in position, every fin extended as in life attitude; the flesh, liver and alimentary canal intact – and even colour on the skin.
* Areas "packed full of splendidly preserved fishes" are found in Ohio, Michigan, Arizona, California and many other places.[3]
* It is estimated that at Lompoc, California, one billion fish perished in four square miles, along with various types of birds.[4]

* In the Rockies, masses of trilobites and other delicate fossils are perfectly preserved – as are RIPPLE MARKS – suggesting not gradual but SUDDEN catastrophic burial.

Europe
* *Scotland:* An area of sandstone covering half of Scotland was investigated by geologist Hugh Miller. He reports that "a thousand different localities" reveal the same violent destruction. A particular area covering at least 10,000 square miles and containing fossil fish was described by Miller as having been exposed to a major destructive force. The rocks in this area are "strewed thick with remains, which exhibit unequivocally the marks of violent death. The figures are contorted, contracted, curved; the tail in many instances bent around the head; the spines stick out; the fins are spread to the full as in fish that die in convulsions."[5]
* *Italy:* Concerning fish on Monte Bolca, near Verona, W. Buckland says: "The skeletons of these fish are always entire, and closely packed on one another.... All these fish must have died suddenly.... And have been speedily buried in the calcareous sediment then in the course of deposition. From the fact that certain individuals have even preserved traces of colour upon their skin, we are certain that they were entombed before decomposition of their soft parts had taken place."[6]
* *Germany:* Buckland also describes fish deposits in the Harz Mountains: "Many of the fishes… have a distorted attitude, which has often been assigned to writhing in the agonies of death.... As these fossil fishes maintain the attitude of the rigid stage immediately succeeding death, it follows that they were buried before putrefaction had commenced, and apparently in the same bituminous mud, the influx of which had caused their destruction.[7]

This scene of AGONY and SUDDEN DEATH and ENTOMBMENT is identical in many other places ALL OVER THE WORLD.

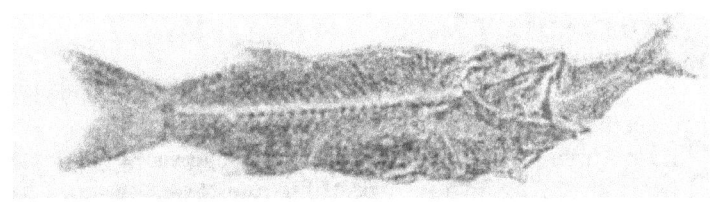

A perch fossilised in the act of swallowing a herring (Wyoming). This suggests rapid burial to preserve the "action" as well as the fossil fish. (Enquiry Press, Michigan, U.S.A.)

The 14 foot skeleton of a large fish which perished while feeding contains a well-preserved 6 foot fish it had just swallowed.

Some large **fish** are found **with LAND** dinosaurs still in their stomachs.

Burrowing shellfish still have their shells (valves) closed, indicating that they did not die a natural death.

All over in 24 hours!

Jellyfish have been found entombed in Cambrian strata. This process, admit geologists, would have to be swift. In fact, it must have been over in 24 hours, or the jellyfish would have disintegrated!

Again, strata in which fish fossils are found actually smell of fish when broken open. Yet when a fish dies in a pond, it has disintegrated within a few days.

The fossilization process must have been rapid and the strata formed rapidly for the preservation of the entire fish and smell!

RAPID FOSSILIZATION

"De la Beche was also of the opinion that most of the fossils were buried suddenly and in an abnormal manner. 'A very large proportion of them,' he says, 'must have been entombed uninjured, and many alive, or, if not alive, at least before decomposition ensued.' In this, he is speaking **not of the fishes alone, but of the fossiliferous deposits in general.**"[8]

Did you notice that? This situation applies to most of the fossils found on this planet!

SEA AND LAND LIFE MIXED TOGETHER, FAR INLAND

On all continents, bones of SEA animals and LAND animals are found **together in great melees**.

* East Africa's Tendaquru dinosaur beds alternate with seashell beds, just as one would expect if a catastrophe swept in from different sources.
* England's Channel Coast: Sea shales and limestones cycle with dinosaur-bearing land deposits.
* Wyoming, U.S.A.: Aralia leaves appear with fish in Cretaceous rocks.
* Oklahoma, U.S.A.: Sea creatures and land plants fill an asphalt pit near Sulphur.

Frequently, remains of WHALES and other monsters and **DEEP-SEA** specimens of life are found far removed from the sea, MIXED WITH **LAND** plants, trees and land animals.

It is common knowledge that the deep floor of the ocean is so calm as never to have its ooze disturbed by the most violent surface storm.

Only some **violent upheaval** such as the biblical Flood, in which "the fountains of the great deep [were] broken up", would explain the MIXTURE of the **deep-sea** specimens with those of shore and land, all covered and preserved by sudden destruction and burial.

SEA LIFE SWEPT ONTO MOUNTAINS

Marine fossils are found on mountain tops hundreds of miles inland from any sea, or buried under hundreds of feet of clay, sand, gravel and other debris.

* Antarctica: Eighty-five mummified seals were found on a mountaintop 2,500 feet above sea level.
* The Himalayas, the world's highest mountains, contain skeletons of ocean fish, molluscs and marine animals. Toward the top of Mount Everest, are petrified clams in the closed position. When a clam dies, it opens. The only way to get a petrified clam in the closed position would be to bury it alive. There are places where clams are found in the closed position and they are piled ten feet thick!

* Fish fossils are found in the Alps of Europe; and oyster fossils are abundant in the Allegheny Mountains.
* Fossil sharks have been found in the Rocky Mountains, entombed by sudden catastrophe; and in the tops of the Canadian Rockies, seashells and even whales – hundreds of miles inland from any seas.
* The South American Andes and the Urals of Russia likewise reveal sea deposits.
* Montreal, Canada: Seals have been found far inland, several hundred feet above sea level.
* Bones and skeletons of whales have been found in hills of Vermont, Montreal, New Hampshire and north of Lake Ontario.
  - Now for the secret of Lompoc's quarry. But first, let me explain about diatoms. These are tiny sea creatures. They say it takes about 1,000 years to accumulate one inch of dead diatoms on the seabed. At Lompoc, the diatomaceous earth is 1,500 feet thick in places. At a diatomaceous-earth quarry in Lompoc, in 1976, a remarkable discovery was made during mining operations. Workers of the Dicalcite Division of Grefco Corporation uncovered the fossil skeleton of a baleen whale. The whale fossil was STANDING ON END in the quarry (well, not quite – it was on an angle of 40 to 50 degrees) and was being exposed gradually as the diatomite was mined. Estimates put the whale fossil at about 80 feet long.[9]

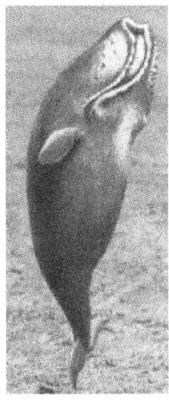

This whale penetrated a diatom formation that, according to evolutionary theory, is millions of years thick. But we all know that a whale skeleton simply would not survive intact for millions of years waiting to get buried while the diatom deposits were slowly forming.

Here, then, was Lompoc's bizarre secret. This baleen whale was the tragic SURPRISE WITNESS to some enormous event. And in this event, diatoms for hundreds of miles around were scooped up and dumped on top of this whale, while the whale itself was being tossed on end. Indeed, it was not just a witness, but a VICTIM of that enormous catastrophe.

This is the "surprise witness" that I selected, to give this current book its title.

Now glaciers don't carry whales. Whales do not stand on their tails. Whales do not climb hills. THE WHALES WERE CARRIED THERE BY RUSHING WATER. Then buried rapidly.

On July 22, 1988, my friend Kent Hovind visited the quarry. And the foreman told Kent, "One time we were digging on the night shift. And we had all the spotlights rigged up. We found a 60-foot wingspan pterodactyl. But we didn't stop and tell anybody, because, if you tell some university, 'We've got a fossil here,' they're going to make you shut down production while they come and dig out their fossil – and you're going to lose money. We're here to make money. And so we just dug right through it."

So, along with this baleen whale and billions of fish fossils, was a giant flying reptile – all caught up in this huge disaster...and now inside a "mountain".

Many mountains on earth show evidence of wave action.

As the Flood waters subsided, they left behind seashells and skeletons of small and large sea creatures scattered over all the present mountain ranges of our planet, including the highest.

FOSSILS PROVE A GREAT FLOOD

Here, then, is the bottom line: fossils in every part of the planet testify to a global Flood.

Sometimes entombed in sediment a mile deep, land and sea forms are mixed together. In America, Europe, Africa, Asia and Australia – in fact, everywhere – they all shout one and the same story.

There was SUDDEN, VIOLENT UPHEAVAL, in which LAND and SEA were mixed up – followed by rapid burial of animals in water-laid sediment, before organisms could decay. This occurred from the North Polar region to the South. It was a catastrophe on a WORLD SCALE.

Only one force known to man is able to perform such a sudden, wholesale destruction, followed by an immediate burial. THAT FORCE IS WATER.

The evolution theory requires that the deposits were formed over millions of years of slow sedimentation. However, I believe the universal Flood fits the facts without difficulty. Judge for yourself.

* * * * * * *

And, in that context, let me tell you about a flight toward the South Pole that gave the crew a mighty BIG surprise…

SEA LIFE CEMETERIES - Summary

FISH: SUDDEN DEATH

Throughout the globe, billions of fossilised fish show indications of violent death. They are found in a pose of agony, with no mark of a scavenger's attack. Their perfectly preserved remains testify to mass burial within hours – not days – of death, before decomposition could occur.

SEA AND LAND LIFE MIXED TOGETHER, INLAND

Frequently, remains of whales and other **deep-sea** creatures are found far removed from the sea, mixed in with land animals, plants and trees.

SEA LIFE ON MOUNTAINS

Marine fossils are found on mountain tops hundreds of miles from any sea, or buried under clay, sand, gravel and other debris sometimes a mile deep.

FOSSILS PROVE A GREAT FLOOD

Fossils in every part of the world testify to a global Flood.

ONLY ONE FORCE KNOWN TO MAN IS CAPABLE OF ACCOMPLISHING A SUDDEN, WHOLESALE DESTRUCTION, FOLLOWED BY AN IMMEDIATE BURIAL. THAT FORCE IS WATER.

9

Coal -
SURPRISE FOR ADMIRAL BYRD

But first, I just have to tell you about that coal-powered train trip. Was on my way to meet a girl on whom I had a hopeless crush. Teenagers do suffer such things, you know. I had decided to summon up courage and ask her to go steady.

Well, I had my head out through the window. And bother it, if coal dust from the engine didn't blow straight into my eye. Talk about irritate! Needless to say, upon arrival in town, I headed first to a doctor. He said the retina might be scratched. I'd better wear a bandage.

So when I got to Jenny's house with that bandage covering half my head, and just one eye to see her with, can you believe it, she laughed so loud I thought they'd hear it in the cemetery. This young man was too embarrassed to ask her out.

Coal!

...More fortunate was that American explorer Admiral Richard Byrd. In 1953, I think it was. From the U.S. base at McMurdo Sound, Byrd was flying toward the South Pole.

Spread out below him in all directions was nothing but empty, endless white. Then they saw it – something quite astonishing, really. The pilot dropped down for a closer look. The object was stark black against all the white. And in the subdued sunlight it glistened, like so many diamond points.

It was a mountain of COAL!

Coal? Here in frigid no-man's land? Coal! Dead vegetation! Near the frozen South Pole? What was it doing here?

COAL

Coal beds are the accumulations of age after age of peat bog growth. Or so the evolution theory tells us. A bog was alternately submerged by the sea, then re-emerged to grow further. The sea rose over it scores of times on the same spot. It must have, because of the different layers of coal.

Let's put this notion to the test. First, let's examine the peat bogs.

Are peat bogs adequate?

According to estimates by coal geologists, it requires from **2 to 20 feet of peat** (vegetable matter decomposed by water and partly carbonised), to compact **into just one foot of coal**.

Geologist Dr. H.G. Coffin, of the Geoscience Research Institute in Berrien Springs, Michigan, offers some interesting facts in relation to the formation of coal beds.

He points out that "the thickness of peat needed to produce one foot of coal depends upon a number of factors." On the basis that "ten feet would be near the average figure,"[1] how tall and thick must a forest be, then, in order to create a seam of coal not one foot thick but 400? The plant remains must be 4,000 feet thick! It would require the compression of a fantastic 4,000 feet of peat!

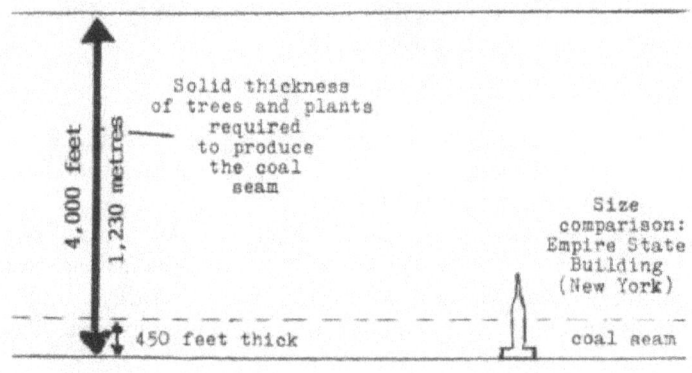

An evolution swamp? 4,000 feet deep? You've got to be kidding.

Coal deposit seams are often 30 or 40 feet thick. Average seams, however, run to 1½ to 10 feet. In Wyoming, one seam is 200 feet thick. An Australian seam (at Yallourn, in Victoria) has a thickness of 450 feet. This means that a solid mass of trees and plants 4,000 feet thick was required to product this one Australian seam! Can you see the problem?

Is such large-scale coal-making taking place today? No. Experts concede that no known present-day marsh, if compressed, would make a large coal seam. The largest coal beds are 100 times thicker than could be derived from the most substantial peat bog.

A respected modern authority concedes that "no single bog or marsh would supply sufficient peat to make a large coal seam."[2]

There are few peat bogs, marshes or swamps anywhere on earth today that attain 100 feet in depth. Most extend but a few feet. If compressed, they would, at best, form only a trace of coal.

Our evolution hypothesis is founded on the theory of uniformitarianism (uniformism) – that the slow, modern natural processes are the key to the past; that nothing different occurred in the past.

Current uniformitarian theories are INADEQUATE to explain the HUGE DEPTHS OF COAL in the earth.

Coal: from ancient forests, not peat bogs

While peat bogs largely comprise sphagnum moss, coal was formed from trees and other large vegetation.

The species mainly were those that don't grow in swamps or peat bogs. The types of trees included the following:

Sassafras	Poplar	Beech	Rosewood
Laurel	Willow	Elm	Plum
Tulip	Maple	Palm	Almond
Magnolia	Birch	Fig	Myrtle
Cinnamon	Chestnut	Cypress	Acacia
Sequoia	Elder	Oak	Kauri
Ironbark	Rimu	Kahikatea	

…. and so on.

These trees were well distributed, worldwide. They all contain **wood** or **leaves**, **flowers** or **fruit**, IN MARVELLOUS PRESERVATION.[3]

Coal is the FORESTS of the ancient world

Coal beds are, then, the forests of the ancient world – the transported and metamorphosed remains of the extensive and luxuriant vegetation of the world before the Deluge.

Just think of it! The vast coal deposits of barren, bleak, icy Greenland and Antarctica **were once steaming jungle THAT WAS TURNED UNDER!**

Pole to pole, vegetation grew in an ideal climate. It is difficult for us today to imagine the enormous amount of vegetation which covered the entire earth. These vegetable materials were washed together in some places to amazing depths.

Not only was the distribution of vegetation superior and different, until the Flood stripped the world of it and buried it as coal, but THE QUANTITY was unbelievable.

Coal deposits in Nova Scotia alone could supply the world with 100 million tons annually for 15,000 years. In North China are coal deposits of 150,000,000,000 tons. Add the rest of the world, and you have the enormous amount of vegetation that was growing when the Flood struck.

Buried suddenly

If coal is not formed rapidly, it does not form at all. Trees or plant debris must be BURIED, COMPRESSED and CUT OFF FROM OXIDATION. Under normal conditions, vegetation would soon decay and merely rot into humus.

Only a SUDDEN BURIAL of HUGE amounts of vegetable material could produce coal. WHOLE FORESTS suddenly buried, forming enormous beds of coal.

Obviously, something extraordinary occurred – suddenly – ON A GLOBAL SCALE.

The evidence is in: these forests were suddenly overwhelmed in some giant cataclysm.

Some trees are positioned with their **tops downward** in the coal (and so could not have grown in place). Violence is implied.

At Swansea Heads, New South Wales, Australia, there are fossilised pine logs which continue **from one coal seam** through 33 feet (10 metres) of sediment **into the next** coal seam.[4]

These logs are well preserved and have **no roots**.

They indicate that the coal they sit in, the sediments which surround the trees, and also the upper layer of coal, ALL FORMED RAPIDLY. The deposits took less time to form than a tree takes to rot.

Polystrate tree trunks near Saint-Etienne, France

Tree trunks that penetrate through several layers of coal or other sediments are known as polystrate tree trunks. One found at Blackroad, Lancashire, measuring 38 feet high is cited in the *American Journal of Science*[5] as evidence of rapid formation. Trees

80 feet long have been found, obviously remaining in place during several tides of sediment deposition.

But a question arises. Why are fossil tree trunks found extending through several successive and separate coal seams, each seam presumably formed during a cycle of millions of years? How could such tree trunks survive these ups and downs while waiting to get buried?

It is evident that the coal layers were buried in QUICK SUCCESSION.

No time to rot!

They have not rotted away. Yet, in some cases, the living tree had only a pithy interior.

Embedded in coal, **boulders of rock** are found – boulders which could only have come from a considerable distance away.

Other objects found in coal include a **gold chain**, an **iron pot** and a **human skull**. These constitute evidence that A HUMAN CIVILISATION PERISHED WHILE THE COAL WAS BEING FORMED.

Professional coal geologists today would acknowledge that coal **had** to form by rapid burial.

Coal CAN form rapidly

It is now possible to scientifically simulate the conversion of wood to coal in the laboratory. We have found that it does not take millions of years. Buried vegetation can change into coal quickly. All it takes is friction and pressure.

Back in the 19th century, a certain bridge was built in Europe, for which large tree trunks were lowered into the riverbed as supporting columns. Over the years, as traffic increased, the superstructure forming the roadway became inadequate for the motorised vehicles, so it was widened and concreted. In due time the bridge was by-passed and a completely new bridge constructed.

When the old bridge was demolished, to the amazement of all concerned, they found that the cores of the old tree trunks had turned to coal! And this within the space of 100 years! The pressure of the load and the heat generated by the vibration of the traffic (and possibly other factors) had contributed to the chemical reactions necessary to convert timber to coal.

In 1882, at Alt-Breisach near Freiburg, Germany, huge blocks of stone were placed over wooden beams. The wood very quickly blackened, until the centre of the beams resembled anthracite, and nearer the surface resembled house coal.[6]

At the 18th Newcastle Symposium (May 1984 Coal Conference), John Mackay and Dr. Andrew Snelling presented field evidence for the role of explosive volcanism in the **rapid** formation of coal seams.[7] Clays appear to play a critical role. They contain minerals which will transform plant debris to coal at temperatures as low as 150°C without the normally assumed requirement of high pressures.

Repeated sequences with marine deposits

Some deposits contain 60, 80, 100 and more successive beds of coal, alternating with sea deposits.

Coal beds in Nova Scotia and New Brunswick are from several thousand to 13,000 feet thick.

Almost universally, one finds between each coal seam layers of waterborne material (shale, sandstone, etc). Often a definite order is repeated dozens of times. In a part of England, for example, the order is:

Fossil-bearing shale

Shale

Sandstone

Fireclay

Clay   ...cycle repeated.

Such regularity seems unlikely if coal was formed by a slow rise and fall of land over millions of years.

To postulate the earth rising and falling on the same spot with successive forest growing and being inundated is a desperate attempt by evolutionary scientists bankrupt for a solution. They are committed to uniformitarian time scales of "millions" of years. And this is their problem.

Evidence shows that some of the vegetation which later became coal FLOATED for a time IN SEA WATER. Fish scales and teeth, mussel shells, calcareous tube worms and other marine organisms are MIXED INTO THE COAL BEDS and often attached to logs in the coal seam. These suggest that ocean water swept the vegetation to its present site.

Also MIXED with the coal are **DEEP** SEA crinoids, clear **SHALLOW** WATER ocean corals and **LAND** boulders.

The physical evidence suggests that the plant matter was washed into place. The coal seams are almost universally found in stratified deposits; the interspersed non-carbonaceous sediments are always said to have been waterlaid. Consistency alone warrants the conclusion that the coal seams were likewise water-deposited.

There have been found in the coal seams "fragments unattached to specific trees and actually **transported** into place by water currents".[8]

Studies of coal beds in India actually admitted that "the vegetation is considered to be drift accumulation".[9]

In the La Trobe Valley in Victoria, Australia, is one of the largest brown coal deposits in the world. Interestingly, it contains a large amount of pine tree material (which could NOT grow in swampy conditions required by the "swamp environment" theory of coal formation).

Also, this coal sits on a layer of white clay. There is no evidence of soil, therefore it could not have been a swamp. This, plus the "jumbled" character of the pine log accumulations, is consistent with its being the product of catastrophic flooding which deposited the clay, then dumped logs and plant material on top of the clay.

Coal from "floating forests"

Entomologist/paleontologist Dr. Joachim Scheven, of Munich, has single-handedly amassed the world's biggest collection of "living fossils". This former evolutionist has worked as a research biologist, has discovered and described several new insect species, both living and fossil, and has published several technical papers, including one on petrified **coal balls**.

Dr. Scheven declares that his research on coal layers in Europe and North America shows irrefutably that these root-like structures did **not** 'grow in place' over millions of years in swamps, but were indisputably structures of the sort found in modern **floating** plants.

THESE WERE NOT ROOTS IN SOILS. The root structures of these floating plants are quite unlike soil-growing roots.

Polystrate tree in the Blue Mountains, New South Wales, Australia (Creation Research)

Here is a question for the "long ages" evolutionist: How did so many coal layers – which had not grown in place – accumulate upon each other?

Only one answer makes sense: they must have been transported, and the transport of plant matter that did not decay must have taken place extremely rapidly.

One volcanic explosion on May 18th 1980 at Mount St. Helens flattened 150 square miles of forest in six minutes. In nearby Spirit Lake millions of logs were catastrophically deposited. Many had their balls of earth around their roots and they eventually sank to the floor of the lake in apparent growth positions. Vegetation mats suffered the same fate and sank to the floor as activity continued. By August 1985 a multi-layered deposit of peat over 3 feet thick was ready to turn to coal upon further burial.

One of the most important clues required to solve the puzzle of coal formation was provided by Karlweil in 1965 and Hill in 1972, who formed coal artificially under conditions similar to volcanism and tectonism.

Then, in 1984, after Mt. St. Helens had erupted, the Argonne National Laboratories in Illinois, U.S.A. produced coal from simple heating of wood in 28 days. They combined wood, water and acidic clay. Heating it in a sealed container (with no added pressure) at 150 degrees Celsius for 28 days, they obtained good grade black coal.

They discovered that in the presence of volcanically produced clays as catalysts, as well as acidic fluids, typical of volcanic and hydrothermal environments, wood turned to coal in periods ranging from 2 weeks to 1 year. Good grade coal formed in four weeks and high grade coal in 8 months.[10]

The conclusion is that coals formed catastrophically under volcanic conditions. And we know that volcanism was a major factor in the Global Flood.

I have in my possession photographs taken by Australian scientist John Mackay in the Birmingham (Warrior Creek) coalfields, U.S.A. Hundreds of trees were discovered poking at all angles out of and through the coal seams. Many of them start from underneath the coal, proceed through the coal and poke through the other side. This shows the trees did not grow from the coal bed material, such as in a swamp. Moreover, many of them have no roots. It also shows that the material forming the coal beds was washed into place quickly before the trees could rot.

The size of the coal beds throughout Alabama indicates that massive quantities of water and debris were involved – something on the scale of a massive watery catastrophe like the Great Flood.

Catastrophe on a continental scale, worldwide

The world's coal fields show overwhelming evidence of catastrophe on a continental scale throughout the world.

Noah's Flood has left its autograph everywhere.

ONLY A WATER DISASTER COULD HAVE DONE IT

This much is certain. No modern day processes can compare with the forces which created earth's immense coal and oil fields. Only a cataclysmic plow could have churned up this much material under the earth's crust.

Water alone could:
1. uproot existing vegetation;
2. drift it together in great heaps; then
3. bury it before it rotted.

The currents and recurring waves of a Flood-tossed ocean can explain why coal seams and layers of other rock are found in repeated sequences and such regular order.

As hurricanes uprooted the forests (some of them fiercely burning), tidal waves fell upon them and swept them into huge heaps, tossed by currents, and covered them with marine sand, shells and pebbles, fishes and weeds. Another tide deposited on top of this mess more logs, often carbonised, tossed them in heaps and covered them once more with marine sediment.

COAL GIVES A POWERFUL TESTIMONY FOR THE DELUGE.

The Deluge provided the MAGNITUDE and SPEED with which to produce coal, oil and natural gas.

However, the question may arise, could so much coal as we have today, have come from only one generation of trees? Surely many disasters would be needed to produce such a vast quantity.

Very well. Let's consider this.

COAL - Summary

EVOLUTIONIST'S EXPLANATION
Coal beds are the accumulations of age after age of peat bog growth. So evolutionists conjecture. A bog was alternately submerged by the sea, then re-emerged to grow further. The sea rose over it scores of times on the same spot.

A problem with this:
But a question arises. Why are fossil tree trunks found extending through several successive and separate coal seams, each seam presumably formed during a cycle of millions of years? How could such tree trunks survive these ups and downs while waiting to get buried?

PEAT BOGS INADEQUATE
It requires, on average, about ten feet of peat to compact into just one foot of coal. An individual coal seam in Australia is up to 400 feet thick; to produce this one seam would have required a solid mass of vegetation at least 4,000 feet thick.

We find no comparable large scale coal-making taking place today. Current uniformitarian theories are inadequate to explain the huge depths of coal in the earth.

COAL FROM ANCIENT FORESTS
While peat bogs largely comprise phagnum moss, coal was formed from trees and other large vegetation. The species mainly were those that don't grow in swamps or peat bogs. Coal beds are the forests of the ancient world – the transported and metamorphosed remains of the extensive and luxuriant vegetation of the world before the Great Flood.

BURIED SUDDENLY
Under normal conditions, vegetation soon decays and merely rots into humus. Only a sudden burial of huge amounts of vegetable material could produce coal.

ONLY WATER COULD DO IT
Water alone could:
1. uproot existing vegetation;
2. drift it together in great heaps; and
3. bury it before it rotted.

No modern day processes can compare with the forces which created earth's immense coal fields.

The evidence is that these forests were suddenly overwhelmed in a great cataclysm. Only a cataclysmic plough could have churned up this much material under the earth's crust.

THE DELUGE PROVIDED THE MAGNITUDE AND SPEED WITH WHICH TO PRODUCE COAL, OIL AND NATURAL GAS.

10

Successive forests – and oil -
ONE FLOOD OR MANY?

"It's impossible!" Hank glared at me. "You say that our vast oil and coal reserves all came from ONE flood?"

He shook his head. "Jonathan, it would take many floods a long time apart, to produce that much supply."

To explain, oil and coal come from organic matter – vegetation and animal life. There could not have been so much organic matter buried at the time of the Great Flood.

It is true that all of today's vegetation, if suddenly turned to coal, would produce only a small proportion of earth's known coal reserves. Therefore, it might be argued, many floods, staggered in time, would be required – not just Noah's Flood.

And that's what my friend Hank was trying to say.

Certainly, if the pre-Flood world was the same as our world today, then that would make very good sense. And I would agree with his reasoning.

However, this is incorrect when one considers the following factors:

1. Most of today's land surface is covered by deserts, sparse vegetation or icy wastes. But coal deposits (for example, in Antarctica) give evidence of a former widespread lush growth of vegetation on this planet.
2. Much former land surface is now under the oceans.[1] This must have carried forests.
3. Compared with our present forests, the ancient climate (again, see Book 1 for details) must have fostered growth beyond comparison.
4. By comparing the stored energy in vegetation with that in coal, it can be calculated that 128 years of plant growth at today's rate

and volume is all that is required to provide the energy equivalent stored in today's known coal beds.[2]

Dr Andrew Snelling couldn't have stated it better:

"Either way, whether by comparison of energy stored in vegetation growth and in coal (i.e. the time factor), or by vegetation growth, climate, geography, land area and compaction (i.e. the volume factor), we can show conclusively that the evolutionist's objection is totally invalid. There was ample time, space and vegetation growth for one Noah's Flood to produce all of today's known coal beds."[3]

PETRIFIED FORESTS

Some forests were covered as they stood, ultimately to become petrified. Whole trees are found in some mines, standing straight up.

Oil drillers in California uncovered the remains of an ancient forest 1,400 feet below the earth's surface.

Petrified trees are further evidence of a global Flood.

Many are found far inland, in deserts, and showing evidence of having been TRANSPORTED from distant parts before they turned to stone – evidence of a big log drift that was left stranded by receding waters.

The "successive forests" of Yellowstone

Evolutionists sometimes quote what they claim is the evidence of some 15 successive forests in Amethyst Mountain and Specimen Ridge, in Yellowstone National Park, U.S.A.

It is argued that it must have taken long ages for these successive forests to grow one after another.

However, a thorough examination of these petrified trees yields some SURPRISES:

1. There is evidence of volcanic activity, interspersed several times with flood water laid sediment.
2. Those so-called petrified forests are in reality only stumps.
3. The root systems are not complete. Only occasional trees remain upright with some parts of the root system still attached.

4. There are no limbs or fossil foliage as one would expect if the complete trees had suddenly been overwhelmed by a shower of volcanic debris.

Many of the trees are in various positions and even prostrate. Other trees apparently remained upright due to the weight of their root systems and attached soil as they were rafted into their final entombment. The appearances do not indicate normal forest growth, but rather catastrophic deposition.

Taking all this into consideration, one is led to conclude that the trees were violently stripped of their branches by some catastrophic force, then washed into place by a succession of strong currents, interspersed with lava flows or volcanic showers from another direction.

The Mount St. Helens eruption provided the proof that such plant deposits can be accumulated exceedingly rapidly.

The result was a mini representation of what is seen through so many coalfields throughout the world.

In 1980, the Mount St. Helens eruption left one million trees stripped of branches floating over 2 square kilometres of nearby Spirit Lake.

Underneath this log mat, as the logs scraped together, the bark fell to the lake bed to form **peat**.

As the logs became water logged, they began to float vertically. Eventually they sank into the layer on the lake floor and produced **what appeared to be twelve separate forests** buried at different layers.

In August 1985, Dr. Steve Austin and other scientists used sonar and scuba to examine the bottom of the lake. They found that about 20,000 of the deposited logs were in **upright position**. Many of these logs still had roots attached to them.

Some were already solidly buried with three feet of sediment around their bases.

The logs were dropping and getting buried at different times, giving the impression of multiple forests – the same feature which appears at Yellowstone and which scientists say must have taken aeons!

At Spirit Lake, it took only five years!

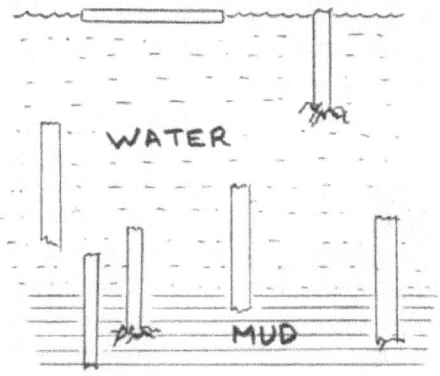

OIL

It is often claimed that oil formation is a process that would require millions of years.

However, oil has been produced in the laboratory from organic material in as little as **twenty minutes!** Oil formation, like that of coal, is not a matter of time, but more of pressure and temperature.

This has been proven recently with the production of oil from household garbage! Annually, "by using the waste-to-oil process, 1.1 billion barrels of oil could be gleaned from the 880 million tons of organic wastes suitable for conversion."[4] In fact, diesel-like fuel is now produced from tropical trees and nuts.[5]

Technology that "mimics nature" is being used in Western Australia, to produce oil "in much the same way that nature produces oil... [but] it is completed in around 30 minutes instead of millions of years."[6]

This proves that millions of years are totally unnecessary, given the right conditions. It is believed that natural oil can form when organic matter deep underground is exposed to raised temperatures.

A.I. Levorsen, in *Geology of Petroleum*, reasons that "the time it takes for oil to accumulate into pools may be geologically short, the minimum being measured, possibly, in thousands or even hundreds of years."[7]

Oil deposits still contain measurable Carbon-14. If they were millions of years old, they should not give a measurement by the Carbon-14 dating method. They have been dated to within the last few thousand years.[8]   If the traditional theory is that they are millions of years old, then the whole concept of carbon dating must be thrown out.

In 1988, it was reported that oil in the Guaymas Basin in the Gulf of California had yielded radio carbon ages of between 4,200 and 4,900 years.[9] The rapid formation of oil and gas had now been shown to take place naturally under geological conditions that have been common in the past.

Oil is the converted remains of organic matter. The existence of oil demands the catastrophic burial of vast numbers of organisms.

Like coal, the existence of oil reservoirs in certain localities must be regarded as a silent witness for a world catastrophe.

As life of every kind was suddenly overtaken, destroyed and buried, sometimes in great heaps, in many instances the oil contained in these millions of bodies was distilled by heat and pressure and filtered out gradually into surrounding strata.

Since then, hydraulic processes have gradually concentrated the oil formed at that time into traps or basins.

The Flood provides the means necessary for such mass burial, in order that oil could form.

Since oil is found on every continent and in every ocean, there is strong scientific evidence for a WORLDWIDE FLOOD.

* * * * * * *

Now, from oil... to people.

Did you hear about the boat discovered inside a mountain, with forty men in it?...

11

Human relics (a) -
LADY BLUE'S LAST VOYAGE

"Lady Blue" was moored at the jetty. Safely, as ever. The river currents were gentle. Always gentle.

...But tonight there was fear in the air. The earth was still shaking. All day this had been going on. Lightning was still leaping from earth to sky. There was a fiendish crackling. Scary.

Throughout the country, the scientists were being asked, "What does it mean? Could Noah be right, after all." The experts spoke soothingly, "There's a good explanation; we're having a conference tomorrow."

Twenty-eight days later, the world was dead. Rain was crashing from the heavens. Volcanoes spat deadly fumes. Skyscraper-high waves, whipped by screaming hurricanes, tore at the mountains.

"Lady Blue", her mast ripped off, was being rocketed forever under water, in a fast-moving current of suspended mud and sand.

This was "Lady Blue's" first and last voyage under the earth.

She stopped suddenly. The rubble continued to pile above her.

Recently she was found – fossilised and in Peru. Miners ran into her, as they dug deep inside the earth.

* * * * * * *

... I watched Carl Sagan being interviewed. Finally the T.V. host asked him, "Now, about creation and evolution: is evolution proved or unproved?"

Replied Sagan:

"The strata of the earth and its FOSSILS show that man hasn't been around very long."

That's it! The proof of evolution is in the fossils.

The earliest life forms appeared, say 600 million years ago. (Thus their fossil remains will be expected in the lower, old rock layers.) But man evolved more recently, say 5 million years old. (So human fossils will be expected only in the higher, more recent layers.)

On the scale of evolutionary time, man is a new-comer.

Now Carl was an able astronomer who popularised his view of science.

But, did you notice, Sagan DID NOT CITE HIS OWN FIELD OF EXPERTISE - ASTRONOMY - to prove evolution… but rather, FOSSILS (paleontology). He knew that no evidence for evolution was to be found in his own field, astronomy. So he assumed that the evidence would be found somewhere else.

That's like a chimney sweep offering you his expertise on Amazon exploration.

So do the fossils and rock layers really prove evolution? In Chapter 14, we shall see what some leading paleontologists (fossil experts) say about this.

Meanwhile, here are some surprises for you.

As we uncover more fossils, we find man consistently appearing PARALLEL with all of his supposed ancestors – not developing from them. We find man consistently present as far back as we go in the fossil record! Human remains are being discovered in the very "oldest" strata, together with the "first and earliest" life forms!

In this chapter I shall introduce you to several dead men who have quite a lot to say to us…

ARTIFACTS
- In Alaska, 90 feet down below the frozen muck and animal remains, a gracefully shaped man-made pink flint **arrowhead** has been found.
- Peru: At Cayatambo, far down at the eighth level, silver miners in 1572 came upon an ancient **nail** embedded in the rock. The 6 inch nail had been riveted to a piece of wood and was totally rust free.[1]
- England: In 1845, the English naturalist Sir Charles Brewster reported to the British Association for the Advancement of Science that a **nail** obviously of human manufacture had been found half-embedded in a granite block excavated from the Kindgoodie Quarry in northern Britain. The granite was "60 million years old." He also

recovered from "75-90 million year old" Cretaceous limestone, **eleven steel nails**.
- Nevada: In 1865, in the Abbey Mine in Treasure City, traces of **a tapered, threaded 2 inch iron screw** were found in feldspar "10 million years old". Though oxidised, the shape of the thread was clearly seen. The San Francisco Academy of Sciences declared: "This discovery could antedate human history by millions of years."
- Pennsylvania: On June 9, 1891, Mrs S.W. Culp in Morrisonville, Illinois, accidentally dropped a shovelful of coal on the floor. One large piece broke open. Inside it was **an intricately made 8 carat gold chain**, 10 inches long, coiled and embedded. When the coal broke into two pieces, the two ends of the chain remained attached, one to each piece of coal. The coal, said to be of the "Carboniferous era," and about 300 million years old, came from a mine in Pennsylvania.[2]
- Tweed, England: Blasted out of a quarry near Rutherford Mills in 1844, emerged **a gold thread** of artificial manufacture. It was inside rock "60 million years old."[3]
- Illinois: In 1851, **two copper rings** were found 117 feet below ground.
- Dorchester, Massachussetts: Also in 1851, a **metallic vase** was blown out of an immense mass of solid rock. The rock was said to be Precambrian, "over 600 million years old." Made of an unknown metal, the artefact was beautifully inlaid with pure silver. It portrayed six figures of a flower, a bouquet, and a vine or wreath. The chasing, carving and inlaying are cleverly and exquisitely done.

(*Scientific American*, Vol.7, p.298, June 5, 1852, reported the actual site as Meeting House Hill. "On putting the two parts together it formed a bell-shaped vessel, 4 ½ inches high, 6 ½ inches in the base, 2 ½ inches at the top and about an eighth of an inch in thickness. The body of this vessel resembles zinc in color, or a composition metal in which there is a considerable portion of silver. On the sides there are six figures of a flower, a bouquet, beautifully inlaid with pure silver, and around the lower

part of the vessel, a vine, or wreath, inlaid also with silver. The chasing, carving and inlaying are exquisitely done by the art of some cunning craftsman. This curious and unknown vessel was blown out of the solid pudding stone, fifteen feet below the surface." Reprinted from the *Boston Transcript*). As is the case with many puzzling finds, the object was circulated from museum to museum, then it vanished. Perhaps it is gathering dust in some curator's dank basement)

- West Virginia: When a young person firing a furnace dropped a large piece of coal, something was seen protruding from it. Chemistry teacher Newton Anderson broke open the coal and discovered inside it a brass bell with an iron clapper. It was seven inches long. A scanning electronic elemental analysis showed it to be composed of brass, bronze and arsenic, sodium and antimony, a composition that could not be reproduced by today's metallurgy technology. The bell could still function well.
- California: Under Table Mountain, Tuolumne County, J.H. Neale discovered a mortar and pestle in a mine tunnel penetrating Tertiary deposits "33 to 55 million years old".

- California: A metal object like a **bucket handle** was discovered inside gold-bearing quartz.
- England: A "**bucket handle**" was found in "10 to 700 thousand year old Pleistocene" stone.
- Austria: In 1865, a **machine-made metal cube** was discovered in coal "from the Tertiary period, 12 to 70 million years old." The discovery was in the foundry of Isidor Braun of Vocklabruck. The edges were perfectly straight and sharp. Four of its sides were flat. The other

two sides opposite each other were convex, and a fairly deep incision ran all the way around its middle. The object was made of hard steel and nickel alloy. Machine-cut, it seemed to be part of a larger mechanism.

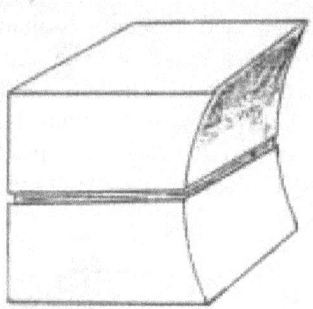

The son of Braun took it to the Linz Museum. It remained in the Salzburg Museum until 1910. It is presently at the Heimathaus Museum, Vocklabruck. Contemporary magazines (for example, *Nature*, London, Nov., 1886 and *L'Astronomie*, Paris, 1887) ran articles about this strange find.[4]

- In mines in the **U.S.A.**, **Italy**, **England**, **Germany**, **France** and **Russia**, a large number of metallic objects with intersecting angles have been discovered. (These are not cylindrical objects, which would be natural.)
- Gulman, Colorado: In 1967, a well-tempered 4 inch **arrowhead** and human bones were found embedded 400 feet down in a vein of silver "several million years old." The discovery was at the Rocky Point Mine in Gulman.[5]
- Thomas, Oklahoma: In 1912, at the Thomas Municipal Electric Plant, fireman Frank J. Kenword split a large piece of coal and discovered an **iron pot** embedded inside. The source of the coal was the Wilburton, Oklahoma, Mines. The pot, now on display at the Miles Musical Museum in Eureka Springs, has been examined by thousands of curious people.[6]

- Saint-Jean de Livet, France: A man-made metallic tube was found in a "65 million year old" chalk bed.

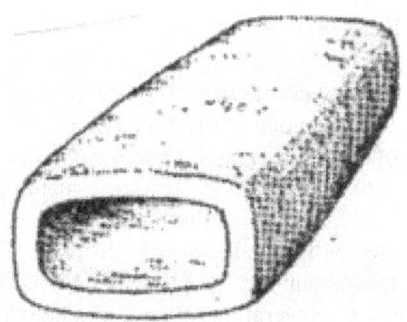

- Aix-en-Provence, France: In 1786-88, fifty feet underground below eleven beds of compact limestone, coins, tools and stumps of columns were found.[7]
- Glasgow, Scotland: A **"modern" iron instrument** was found in a coal bed "260 to 340 million years old."
- Illinois: At Chillicote, **bronze coins** were found 137 feet below ground.

- Oklahoma: In 1926, at Wilburton, miners dug up a **solid block of silver carved in the shape of a barrel**.
- England: At Chute Forest near Stonehenge and also at Westerham, Kent, **coins** have been discovered inside masses of flint.
- Colorado: An **iron thimble** was found in a coal seam "70 million years old."[8]
- Pennsylvania: A **spoon** was found inside coal.[9]

"What!" I hear someone exclaim, "Surely not!! Man on earth before the coal was formed???! No, no, this cannot be! Our evolution theory..."

Evolution? Hmm...

A PRE-FLOOD HAMMER ANALYSED

*   London, Texas: A **metal hammer** was uncovered in Ordovician sandstone during quarrying in June 1934 and the fossil shells surrounding the hammer were dated on the evolutionary time scale as at least 400 million years old.[10]

This story is a fascinating one.

Above the Llano Uplift granite, the Ordovician sandstone was being quarried back. In the process, an internal concretion was exposed. It aroused interest immediately because of the piece of wood poking out. This was anomalous. According to the theory of gene pool expansion, wood had not evolved by the Ordovician period.

When the concretion was split open, the wood was revealed to be the handle of an iron hammer. There are two things that everyone agrees upon. Firstly, the concretion and associated fossils are of Ordovician age. Secondly, the hammer is genuine. The only question was whether or not the hammer had been locked into the strata at the time the strata formed. Several important clues help here.

There is a contraction zone around the iron head that typically forms as rock hardens. This indicates that the hammer fell into sediments while they were still soft. The hammer has bevelled edges and ends. A small sample of iron was scratched from the surface for analysis. The iron contained an unusual amount of chlorine. This indicated a manufacturing process with which we are unfamiliar. Furthermore, the handle was partially turned to coal in the centre and contained fluid inclusions.

This evidence required the hammer to have been impacted under heat and fluid pressure, seemingly at the time the strata was formed. If this is in fact the case, then mankind must have been there when the Ordovician was laid down.

The composition of the hammer head has been investigated using sophisticated scanning electron microscopy (S.E.M.) equipment. This research on the distribution of chemical substances within the hammer head was performed by the highly-respected Batelle Laboratories in the U.S.A.

So why are the results so mysterious?

They are surprising because the hammer head, which is made of iron, appears to contain none of the minor quantities of substances such as silicon or carbon which are normally incorporated in modern iron and steel production. According to the Batelle report, the hammer head contains no silicon, no nickel and no carbon whatsoever.

The analysis (semi-quantitative) by weight shows that the hammer is made of 96.6% iron, 2.6% chlorine and 0.74% sulphur – a most unusual situation. Since it has no carbon, it is not steel in the modern sense. It has no silicon, therefore it does not appear to have been formed by any known modern means of furnace production for steel and the presence of such a high percentage of chlorine is strange indeed.

Producing steel or iron in any modern heating furnace always adds silicon to the end product, even if only in minor quantities. This hammer head contains absolutely no silicon.

While modern steels are made using carbon, it has been known for quite a while that it is possible for carbon in a steel to actually leak out of the steel over time and leave no trace. However, no process is known, according to the metallurgists we consulted, whereby silicon could have moved out of the iron head and left no trace.[11]

This pre-Flood hammer is presently in the possession of Dr. Carl Baugh of Glen Rose, Texas.

SHIPS COVERED BY MOUNTAINS

The buried remains of large, well-formed boats or ships, have also been found, either in solid stone or at remarkable depths underground in Switzerland.[12]

The Swiss discovery occurred in 1460 when miners were digging for metals in the canton of Berne. The ship was buried 100 feet deep inside the mountain. There was an anchor of iron. But what horrified the miners was the sight in the timbers of the bones and skulls of forty men.

One can just imagine the mockers of Noah who believed not in that coming disaster. "Anyway, we have boats," I hear them saying. "We can save ourselves." And as the Deluge sweeps over the land, some head out to sea, to escape the carnage. But then they too are overwhelmed – and the weight of a mountain is piled over them.

And now to Naples, Italy. In the 16th century, after an earthquake split open a mountain, a large ship was found inside the mountain.

Down to Peru, in South America. About the year 1540, near Callao, Spanish miners were following a vein of gold and silver. There, deep underground, they were startled to come upon an ancient ship.[13]

Ovid likewise speaks of ancient ship anchors found on the tops of the highest mountains.

BUILDINGS AND INSCRIPTIONS
* Western Australia: In 1975, water drillers 80 miles from Perth struck concrete 30 feet below the surface. Investigation proved

the existence of a **concrete wall**.
* France: At Aix-en-Provence, from 1786 to 1788, **coins**, stumps of **columns** and other worked stones, were discovered 50 feet down, below eleven beds of compact limestone.
* Kentucky: At Blue Lick Springs, underground, below the remains of a prehistoric mastodon, was discovered a **pavement of cut-stone tiles**.
* Ohio: In the autumn of 1868, in a strip of coal mine operated by Captain Lucy near Hammondsville, at 100 feet below ground a large mass of coal fell into the shaft, unmasking a **large, smooth, slate wall covered with inscriptions similar to hieroglyphics**, in lines about three inches apart. Crowds flocked to see this marvel. By the time qualified scientists got there with proper equipment, the slate had crumbled in the air and the writing was destroyed.
* Pennsylvania: In November 1829, "in a quarry twelve miles northwest of Philadelphia, at a depth of 69-70 feet below ground, a **block of marble** was found, which bore an indentation containing the **raised alphabet characters** 'I' and 'U'." The discovery was authenticated by several reliable witnesses and two years later an illustration appeared in the *American Journal of Science*, vol.19, p.361.

* Omaha, Nebraska: About 130 feet underground, coalminers found a carved slab of rock. The marks on it divided the shape into diamonds. In the centre of each diamond was an engraving of a human face. The earth had not been disturbed – and the coal was dated at 300 million years.[14]

* Oklahoma: In 1928, in coal mine No. 5, near Heavener, **at a depth of two miles**, miners encountered a **wall** composed of 12 inch cube concrete blocks. The blocks were so smooth and polished on the outside that all six sides acted as mirrors. A solid wall was exposed. About 100 to 150 yards further down the shaft, the same wall or one very similar was uncovered.

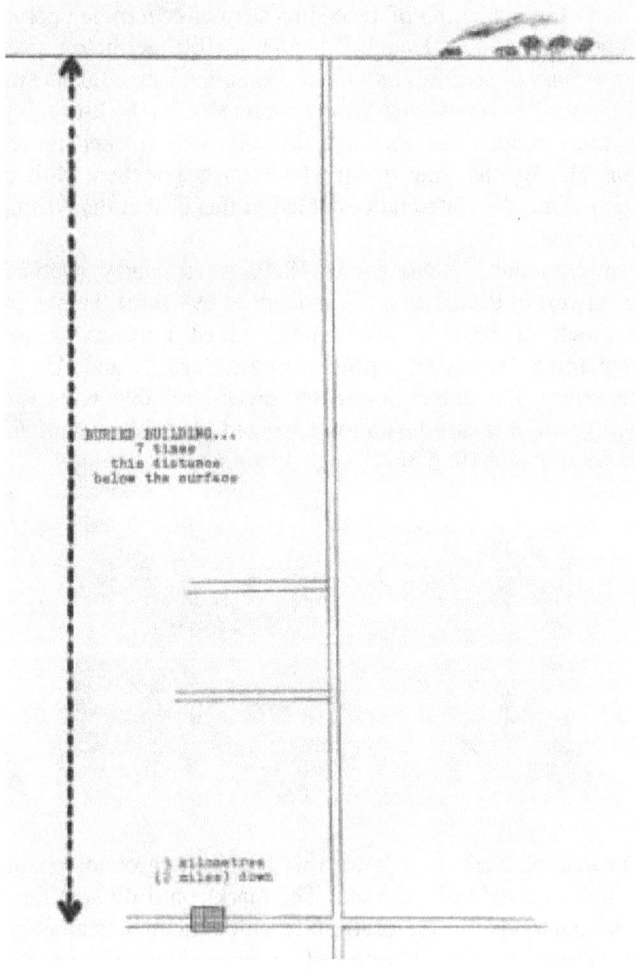

When they reported the discovery to the mining officers, the men were pulled out of that mine and sent to another mine. That part of the mine was then filled up.[15]

What's going on here? Who's afraid these things will get known?

And doesn't it strike you? As deep as two miles (3.2 kilometres) underground! Whatever it was that buried these items could NOT have been a mere flood. We're dealing with a cataclysm beyond understanding!

COVER-UP

How interesting! If something is discovered that fits with established ideas, it is fussed over, put on display and written about extensively. If it challenges the accepted line, then you don't hear much about it, it gets "lost" or it is denied.

You see, there is money involved in the established system. Positions. Reputations. Opportunity for publication. Small and powerful groups control careers.

If you want a university post, you need recommendations. To get your articles published in scientific journals, you must pass what is called "anonymous peer review".

It is easy for a dominant group to control publication, research money and position. If you want to "succeed", you have to go along with them.

I have met victims of that system, who have been denied these privileges, only because of their views.

But let's continue…

12

Human relics (b) -
FOOTPRINTS IN COAL

"It looks like he was trying to escape when the water overtook him. Anyway, I gave the evidence to a the American Museum of Natural History."
"You shouldn't have done that!"
"Why not?"
"Give it some time and they'll deny they ever got it."
You'll learn the sequel to this conversation in a moment.

* * * * * * *

Artefacts are one thing.
But have any traces of actual humans been found where they should not be?
Indeed they have.
But let's start with footprints.
Human footprints are found in undisturbed strata of virtually all geological "ages" – and in rock layers where the "earliest" life forms appear.
Hear are a few examples:
- Gobi Desert (discovered 1959): A print of a ribbed sole (shoe or sandal size 9), in sandstone rock "2 million years old."[1]
- Fisher Canyon, Nevada: A shoe print with clear traces of strong thread, in a coal seam "12 million years old."

Pershing County, Nevada, 1927: A shoe print, showing evidence of a well-cut and double-stitched leather sole, in Triassic limestone "160 to 195 million years old."[2] This find was authenticated by a competent geologist of the Rockefeller Foundation in New York. The thread is smaller than any used by shoemakers today. Samuel Hubbard, honorary curator of archaeology of the Oakland Museum, is quoted as saying, "There are whole races of primitive men on earth today, utterly incapable of etching that picture or sewing that moccasin. What becomes of the Darwinian Theory in the face of this evidence that there were intelligent men on earth millions of years before apes are supposed to have evolved?"[3]

Fisher Canyon shoeprint in a coal seam "12 million years old"

I'll give you another example of the way discoveries such as these are handled. The person who made the Pershing County discovery took it to New York. He took it to Columbia University. He showed it to some of the leading people there at the American Museum of Natural History and turned it over to them. Michael Cremo reports, "We wrote to the American Museum of Natural History and they had no information about it. They said that the report is not in their files."[4] How convenient.

- Nevada: A semi-circular shoe-heel imprint in rock "10 to 27 million years old."
- Cow Canyon, Nevada (25 miles east of Lovelock): The graceful imprint of a well-balanced human in a coal vein of the Tertiary "period."
- England, 1948: A shoe imprint with nail heads around its outer edge, in "450 million year old" limestone.

- Antelope Springs, Utah: Prints of a man wearing shoes, in which the left foot had trodden on a trilobite, a creature of "440 million years ago." Prints included one of a child's foot, with all five toes showing dimly.[5]

This discovery was made in the Wheeler Formation, in the House Range east of Antelope Springs, in shaley limestone rock. On June 1, 1968, William Meister was looking for trilobite fossils. With difficulty, he was climbing a 2000 ft high rock face. He paused, and broke off a 2 inch thick lump of rock with his geology hammer. It opened like a book, revealing a trilobite in the heel of a sandal print. A consulting geologist was called in. He found more sandal-prints and some footprints of bare-foot children. It would seem from this evidence that mankind and trilobites co-existed.

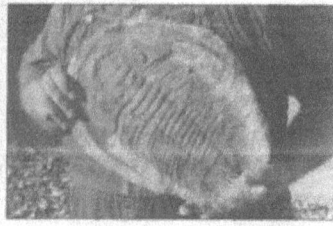

Left: A sandalled foot worn by a human crushed this trilobite while it was alive. The Trilobite era is alleged to be "300 million years ago". Right: A larger trilobite fossil

- Laetolil, Africa: Footprints in rock "12 million years old."[6]
- Tulsa, Oklahoma: Footprints in rock "12 million years old."[7]
- Carson City, Nevada: Sandal prints in Pliocene "age" rock "12 million years old."[8]
- Glen Rose, Texas: Footprints in Cretaceous rock "70 million years old."[9]
- Mt. Victoria, Australia: Footprint in Triassic rock "200 million years old."[10]

- St. Louis, Missouri: Footprints in Permian rock "200 million years old."[11]
- Bera, Kentucky: Footprints in Pennsylvanian rock "200 million years old."[12]
- Lake Windermere, England: Sandal print in Ordovician rock "400 million years old."[13]

One could go on. Examples are becoming almost countless.

Evolutionary theory in trouble

There's something wrong here. Do you see? If human footprints in ancient rocks are genuine, then either men existed before evolution stipulates they should, or our geological dating systems are in serious error.

I should stress that these prints were found only after removal of overlying rock strata. The impressions were made at a time when the rock was soft enough to receive them by pressure.

Such discoveries are a serious contradiction of evolutionary geology. As James Madsen, curator of Earth Science at the University of Utah, stated for the press, concerning the trilobite-with-man find:

"There's something of a problem here, since trilobites and humans are separated by millions of years" (in theory, over 200 million!).[14]

Indeed, this intimate simultaneous occurrence of modern (sandal-shod) man with "primitive" trilobites **is** a serious problem for the evolution theory.

Evolution? Quite the opposite.

Could these "footprints" be fakes?

I should mention that there have been desperate attempts to discredit such tracks. However, there is no denying that many of them were found "inside" stratified deposits, where forgery was impossible.

I shall repeat, the impressions were made at a time when the rock was soft enough to receive them by pressure.

As Ivan T. Sanderson points out, the vast majority of the impressions "were not discovered 'on the top of' or 'outside of' slabs of either sedimentary strata, or on on-sedimentary boulders... These human-type imprints... came to light when the rocks were being quarried, and they were found on the surfaces of laminae [layers] 'inside' said stratified deposits – and in some cases, dozens of feet below the present surface and hundreds of yards back into the quarries. [If these footprints are hoaxes] how did the funsters get them into solid rock a hundred feet down and a hundred feet in from a quarry face; and then arrange for some fellow to split just the right two laminae apart – in the presence of witnesses, mind you – to disclose the hilarious fake. Come on, skeptics; can't you do better than that?"[15]

Independent and meticulous examination of fossil human footprints by a number of scientists has confirmed that "the sand grains within each track are closer together than the grains immediately outside the tracks and elsewhere on the rock... due to the pressure of the creature's foot." This is a characteristic of genuine footprints.[16]

Writing in *Scientific American* concerning footprints in Carboniferous rock, Albert C. Ingalls states:

"If man, or even his ape ancestor, or even that ape ancestor's early Mammalian ancestor, existed as far back as in the Carboniferous Period in any shape, **then the whole science of geology is so completely wrong** that all the geologists will resign their jobs and take up truck driving. Hence for the present at least, science rejects the attractive explanation that man made these mysterious prints in the mud of the Carboniferous Period with his feet."[17]

There you have it. A frank admission that the facts are being deliberately sidestepped.

So what do these tracks tell us?

This much is certain. To be perfectly preserved, the tracks had to be covered ALMOST INSTANTLY. They were then buried under hundreds of feet more of earth.

The person who squashed the trilobite may have taken only a few more steps before the Great Flood wiped him out.

As notes Dr. Burdick: "These tracks... were preserved in rock hundreds of feet below the present surface of the ground, as though at or near the beginning of some great catastrophic, earth-shaking event that buried many forms of life all together, some marine and some non-marine."[18]

Here is evidence of catastrophe... and also of mankind as far back as the Precambrian ("before the first life on earth") period.

What does THAT mean?

Okay, let's go beyond footprints. How about some real people? Let's see...

13

Human relics (c) -
MEN IN EMBARRASSING PLACES

"I'd never be caught dead in a coal mine," drawled Paul.

He was an immaculate dresser, obsessed with cleanliness. In fact, he would never soil his hands in the garden. Let alone enter a black, dusty coal mine.

Paul didn't need to. He was born with a silver spoon in his mouth.

Some others of us had to work hard to survive. And that doesn't hurt anyone.

But I want to introduce you to some men who WERE caught dead in a coal mine – or mines (plural), to be precise.

Whatever they did for a living, I have no idea. Some may have been attorneys, or farmers, or chefs. But they all died in a violent manner and ended up with forests of trees washed over them – which eventually turned to coal... which in recent times would be mined.

"In all the wrong places"

These are human remains "in all the wrong places."

In the last chapter, we noticed some man-made objects inside coal. And this prompted us to ask, was man on earth BEFORE the coal was formed?

But even worse – if that's possible – are some real, physical discoveries of human parts in coal seams!

* Billings, Montana, November 1926: In the Number 3 Eagle Mine at Bear Creek, a tooth, declared by dentists to be the second lower molar of a human being, was found in "70 million year old" Eocene coal.[1]
* Italy: In 1958, a human skeleton was found in a mine, the coal of which was "11 million years old."[2]
* Freiberg, Saxony: "In the coal collection in the Mining Academy in Freiberg, there is a puzzling human skull composed

of brown coal and manganiferous and phosphatic limonite, but its source is not known. This skull was described by Karsten and Dechen in 1842."[3]

* Tuscany, Italy, 1958: Professor Johannes Hurzeler of the Museum of Natural History in Basil, Switzerland, found in a "10 million year old" lump of Miocene coal the jawbone of a child flattened like a piece of sheet iron.[4]
* Dr. Henry Morris reports having interviewed a coal miner in West Virginia who had found a perfectly formed human leg that had changed into coal.
* Castenedolo, Italy, 1860: Skulls of two children, a man and a woman of the "modern" type, were found in undisturbed Pliocene strata "at least 12 million years old."[5]
* Olmo, Italy, 1863: Another similar find was made in Pliocene strata.
* Calaveris, California, 1886: A skull identified as unmistakenly human was found in the middle of a mountain, likewise in Pliocene strata.[6]
* Moab, Utah, May, 1971: Lin Ottinger found teeth and parts of two skeletons of "Homo sapiens" ("modern" man) inside a geological stratum "100 million years old." This find has been well documented.
* Gilman, Colorado: A human skull was found in Cretaceous strata "70 million years old."[7]
* La Sal, Utah: Two more skeletons in Cretaceous strata.
* Macoupin County, Illinois: A human skeleton found in 1862 in a coalfield of the Carboniferous period was reported in *The Geologist*, a standard journal. It was in rock up to "300 million years old."
  * Franklin County, Mo.: A human skeleton was found in Silurian rock "300 million years old."[8]

And these are just the start. Did you know that hundreds and hundreds of "modern" human skeletons have been discovered in rock that dates back more than "100 million years?"

MEN WITH DINOSAURS?

Popular theory is that dinosaurs died out 65 million years ago and that mankind emerged but "recently" as evolution's most advanced product.

But what if man and dinosaur emerged together?

- Palaxy River basin, near Glen Rose, Texas: In 1908, dinosaur and human footprints were found TOGETHER – and photographed.

  In 1982 and again in 1984, Drs. Clifford Wilson (formerly Director of the Australian Institute of Archaeology) and Dr. Carl Baugh of Texas removed a bed of solid Cretaceous limestone to uncover more of these prints. The sequence of left-right footsteps along with the dinosaur prints went towards a rock outcrop that sat on top of that stratum with the prints.

  Dr. Wilson pointed out that if the tracks were genuine, and not just clever carvings, they should continue in this very same stratum that went on underneath the rock layer or step. He set his team to work and removed this superimposed rock layer. Both the man tracks and the dinosaur prints continued on!

  Wilson reports: "The Press and Scientists were invited to watch what was taking place, and although the Press came in considerable numbers – and reported favourably – evolutionary scientists did not come until about a year later when they were able to show that the footprints were erosions in the stone – which of course they were by that time! However the Press personnel present were able to video-tape as footprints of both dinosaurs and humans were uncovered, and I personally have casts in my possession which truly demonstrate that human footprints were indeed found alongside dinosaur footprints..."[9]

Oh, and something else. A trilobite usually dated at about 250 million years ago was also found in the same stratum.

In this very same stratum, there are at least 70 human footprints and 478 dinosaur tracks – yes, together in the same stratum.

These were found after uncovering undisturbed strata. A number of these are distinct trails – right foot, left, right, etc. They not only have the normal left-right human stride, but also the angled toes, the arch, ball and heel.

Human tracks cross dinosaur tracks (courtesy www.bible.ca)

Child, adult and giant prints cross the dinosaur trails. The adult and child prints form a snug fit for the many parents and children who 'try them on for size'.

Some human-like tracks actually overlap dinosaur tracks. There is no doubt that the man who left these tracks saw a living dinosaur.

A human footprint superimposed onto a dinosaur track

Says Dr. Burdick: The stride of the giant human tracks was about six feet, "until the fellow started to run, when the stride lengthened to nine feet, when only the balls of the feet showed, with no toes. Then the series of tracks disappeared into the bank."[10]

Evidently, these strata were laid down during the first few days of the Flood, when water levels were low enough to allow daily tidal changes to form layers of mud, which covered the tracks of creatures seeking higher ground. The upper strata showed no prints.

The debate begins

Many of the human prints were detached from their position and put on show. But these had insufficient documentation for general acceptance, and those left in place after initial exposure always suffered from extreme erosion, removing any distinctive features necessary to identify them.

At least one of the trails was over-enthusiastically identified as human. The skeptics correctly denied these as valid evidence and other creation scientists rejected them also. The evolutionists, have however, most commonly ignored the tracks, or have superficially examined older, eroded tracks, and thus found no compelling evidence to declare them human. They have undertaken no serious excavations of their own.

Nevertheless, a number of other excavators - such as Dr Tom Patton on September 9, 2000 - have independently uncovered separate sets of dinosaur/with man tracks. This kills the objection that the earlier-found tracks were not authentic.

More systematic work is starting to amass an impressive array of *in situ* specimens for further scientific evaluation. These include the undeniable ancient print of a human hand in the same dinosaur track stratum.

Destroying some evidence

On August 12, 1989 Dr. Don Patton spoke at a conference in Dayton, TN. He presented compelling evidence, with pictures, that both human and dinosaur tracks were present at what is known as the Taylor Trail.

Two well known evolutionists were present. And at least one was conspicuously disturbed by this presentation. Both flew to Dallas the next morning and went immediately to the Paluxy River.

It is reliably reported that they were in the river that afternoon with an "iron bar." Three days before they were in the river a series of photographed footprints was observed looking normal. Three days after they were in the river, it was observed and photographed in a state of destruction.

Pointing the finger

In the mid 1980s a landowner was quarrying for road gravel. And inside the quarry he uncovered a fossilized human finger!

Medical doctor Dale Peterson of Oklahoma City examined the sectioned specimen by means of x-ray, CT Scan and MRI. He was able to identify joints and to trace tendons throughout its length. He announced, "There can be no reasonable doubt that this is a fossil finger."

In fact, the soft tissue was fossilized and preserved with remarkable detail. Dr. Peterson reports, "The fingernail and cuticle were clearly visible and perfectly formed and proportioned. The fossil was not of uniform or random density and coloration. The internal appearance of the fossil was identical to what one sees when a human finger is sectioned. The skin margins and subcutaneous tissue were clearly delineated. The bone matrix was clearly defined, and features consistent with flexor and extensor tendons were present."

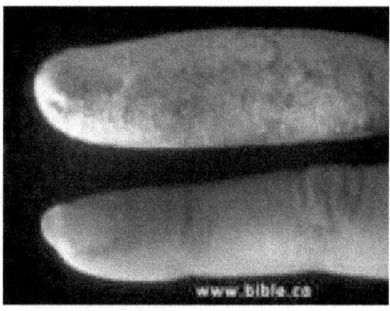

This is indeed the finger of someone who was rapidly buried in a catastrophic event long ago.

I have also spoken at length with Ed Conrad, another explorer of coal strata from the so-called "dinosaur age". He also has found unmistakeable human remains, including a skull with teeth present, and a human finger.

Twenty medical experts have pronounced this as a genuine human finger. This is not good news for the evolution theory.

Honestly, you have no idea of the banning, the deceit and vilification to which men like Ed Conrad are subjected. If such finds cannot be ignored, they will be denied, discredited or yes, even physically destroyed. I have collected enough evidence of such things to fill a book. But that can wait.

A human tooth with dinosaurs

On Tuesday, June 16, 1987, at the Glen Rose, Texas, site, a human tooth was found in a layer of marl (clay and sand). This layer separated two layers of Cretaceous limestone, both of which contained dinosaur prints.

It was simultaneously discovered by Dr. Carl Baugh of Glen Rose, Mary Lou Del Mul of Plano, Texas, Melinda Crews of Lubbock, Texas and Rick Tingle of Tyler, Texas. Assisting at the site was Bob Helfinstine of Minneapolis, Phillip Isett and Joe Crews of Lubbock, Texas, as well as several other volunteers.

The team had worked several hours to remove a piece of top layer, about 7 feet long by 2 feet deep and 16½ inches thick. This enabled them to explore an area of the next layer in which they hoped to find a continuing trail of either the previously explored dinosaur or human-like tracks.

They then began to carefully remove the clay marl. As one person trowelled the surface material away, he customarily had three observers stationed around him to witness and document any find.

At this moment, Melinda was on the right, Mary Lou on the left and Rick Tingle immediately in front.

Both Rick and Melinda saw the shiny black object in a tiny crevice opened up by the trowel and immediately stepped forward for a closer look.

"It looks like a kernel of corn," said Rick. "Could be a piece of dinosaur claw."

Dr. Baugh carefully picked it up. "It's a tooth!" he exclaimed

It was carefully put back into the depression.

"We must photograph this where it is," said Baugh. "Mike?"

Mike Reddick, the photographer, was from Arlington, Texas. He quickly recorded the event.

The presumed tooth was within 3½ feet of one of the dinosaur prints in the layer below. A human-like print was also nearby, within one foot of the dinosaur track.

Phillip Isett, a soil scientist of West Texas State University at Canyon, Texas, examined the site and concluded that the tooth was found in material which had been undisturbed by intrusion or other sources of contamination.

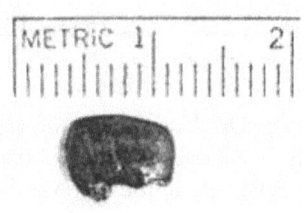

"Tooth" – front view. There is a chip on the right corner and a crack on the face. The root on the left side does not seem completely resorbed, but has been cracked.

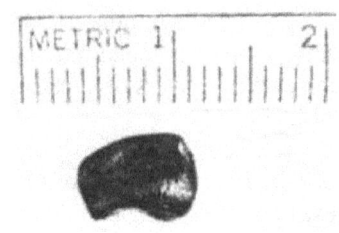

Rear of the "tooth". Note the concave surface, so characteristic of human teeth. The chip is on the left corner.

Dr. James H. Addison, DDS, of suburban Dallas, was the first dentist to examine the tooth. He said that the size of the tooth (7.9mm) was within the extreme range for a human juvenile, listed in the standard texts as between 6 and 8 mm. Dr. Ken Hogan, DMD, from Washington University, of Fort Smith, Arizona, examined the tooth on Wednesday, June 24, and also concluded that its owner was human. Dr. Richard Neal of Fort Worth, Texas, examined the tooth and admitted that he had fully expected to see an animal tooth that had fooled these "non-dentists", but stated that there was no doubt in his mind that this was human.

The dentists were unanimous that it was the deciduous maxillary right central incisor of a human juvenile. Based on the known rate of maturation today, and assuming it was a human tooth, the dentists placed the age of the original owner of this tooth at between 3 and 7 years of age. In popular language, this was the right upper front baby tooth. It was considered not ready to fall out, but was knocked out by some kind of violence. This was further attested by a chip on the left corner and a crack on the front face.[11]

Baugh, who is Director of the Creation Evidences Museum at Glen Rose, called a press conference on June 24. At the press conference, Walter Best, an industrialist from Indianapolis, stated that he was standing with one foot on a DINOSAUR track, another on a HUMAN track, and within five feet of the points of discovery of both a TRILOBITE and a HUMAN TOOTH.

With these, a trilobite!

The trilobite had been found by Dr. Baugh, and witnessed by John Devilbiss and Hugh Miller... in February the same year.

It was at a point 4 feet from the tooth and in the same stratum. It was one of the most complete specimens of trilobite unearthed anywhere.

Significance of the finds

YOU SEE THE IMPORTANCE OF THIS, of course? According to the well-entrenched evolutionary theory, we should find a gradual progression of life forms, starting from the bottom of the earth's rock layers. The so-called "simple" ones are expected to be found at the bottom.

Trilobites, we're told, lived 570- to 230 million years ago, then died out. So when trilobites are found in a rock, they are an index to the age of the rock. And rocks are dated accordingly.

Long after that, dinosaurs evolved. They ruled the planet 135- to 65 million years ago.

Man appeared 5- to 1 million years ago.

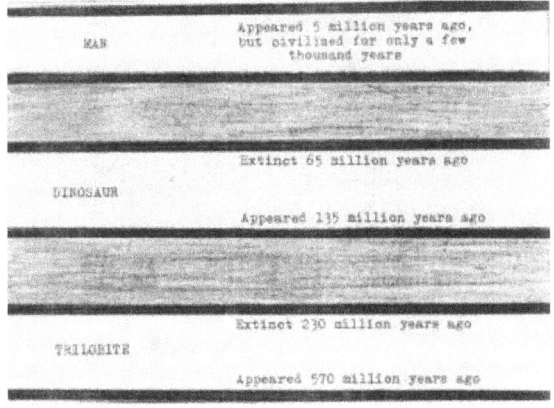

So goes the theory – hammered into our children at school, pushed through the universities, sneaked to us through the media... taken for granted as fact.

Man's presence will be found near the top layers of the earth, because man was a late comer.

If you believe what you read in the newspapers, hear on the radio or see on T.V., then evolution is not a theory but a fact. They tell us that we must rid ourselves of the idea that ALL forms of life appeared together as a planned creation – or that dinosaurs, trilobites and men were contemporary with each other. You must not fall for that myth of a Flood that deposited most of these creatures in the rocks in one big event.

Indeed, the evolution status quo makes us feel comfortable. That is, until we go after the HARD EVIDENCE.

Then comes that sinking feeling. Could it be that an enormous mistake has been made?

Glen Rose, Texas. Look what's found:

Main ledge	Several dinosaur prints	HIGHER
Clay layer	In close proximity: A trilobite and a human tooth	
Next Limestone layer beneath	In close proximity: 3 three-toed dinosaur prints in stride (2 left & 1 right) and a man "track"	LOWER

THE SITE IS CONSIDERED TO BE CRETACEOUS
("110 million years" old)

Now think! If one trilobite were found in situ with one human tooth, then the whole scheme of evolution would be in ruins. The result would be to COMPRESS INTO SIMULTANEOUS TIME ALL THE GEOLOGICAL EPOCHS from the Permian (230 years ago – the last accepted trilobite) to the Pleistone (5 million years ago – the alleged first evidence of modern man).

Other locations
* The findings of scientists uncovering dinosaur prints and related human prints have been verified by similar human/dinosaur print combinations in Australia and Turkmenia.[12]
* Florida: A skeleton of a **dinosaur** was found, with an **arrow head** embedded in the skull – evidence that the animal lived and died at the same time as the hunter.
* Near El Boqueron, in the state of Tolima, Colombia: In 1971, Professor Henero Henao Marin was excavating near El Boquerou, in the State of Tolima, when he exposed a 65-foot skeleton of a **dinosaur** next to a **human skull**.[13]
* Under the mountains of California, amidst **dinosaur** bones, have been found actual **human** remains.
  Famous among these is the Calaveras skull, found beneath repeated layers of volcanic rock, at a depth of 132 feet. (We referred to this earlier.)
* Brazil: In excavations at Lagoa Santa and elsewhere in the state of Minas Gerais, **human** skeletons were found buried under bones of the nine-foot toxodon, the twenty-foot megatherium and the **dinosaur**.[14]
* South Australian scientist Dr. Barry Setterfield lists eight locations where the activity of mankind is recorded in Mesozoic (Dinosaur Age) strata.
  Among them are human skeletons found in separate areas within the Dakota Sandstone. In each case, they were about 7 metres below the top of the formation and had been exposed by quarrying operations. When uncovered, the strata went through the bones. This seemingly indicated burial at the time the strata was formed.[15]
* Skeletons of ten "modern" humans have been excavated from 58 feet below the surface in the Dakota Sandstone, in the same formation known for its dinosaurs.
  This formation (found at Dinosaur National Monument) is a member of the Lower Cretaceous, supposedly 140 million years old. At least four of the ten individuals are female. One is an infant.

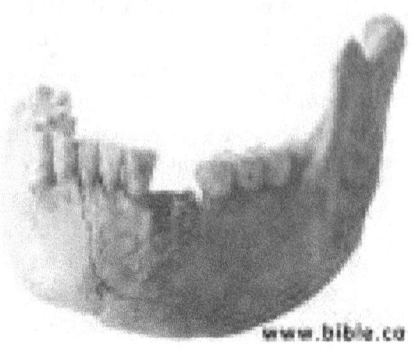

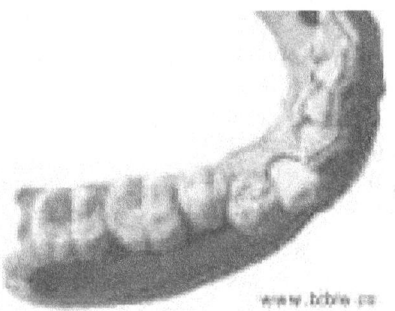

It is evident that these people were buried rapidly by some catastrophe, like a flood. Some of the remains are articulated. This indicates rapid burial.

These humans appear to have been buried by the same catastrophe that buried dinosaurs in this continent-spanning formation.

Humans and dinosaurs must have lived at the same time.

What this means

As you can see, there is a substantial amount of evidence that clearly DESTROYS our popular concepts of organic EVOLUTION and earth history.

Obviously:
1. Man was on earth BEFORE the coal was formed.
2. Dinosaur and man lived at the same time.
3. Man was around in the "EARLIEST" geological periods.

Just compare the two charts on the next two pages.
1. **The theory** (the geological time sequence, taught in our schools)
2. **The facts** ("impossible" human relics in **all** these strata)

This is the theory:

	THE GEOLOGICAL TIME-SCALE		Estimated years ago
QUATERNARY — Age of Man	Recent (Neolithic, Bronze, Iron)		25,000 to 5,000,000
	Pleistocene or Glacial (Paleolithic)		
TERTIARY — CENOZOIC Age of Mammals	Pliocene Miocene Oligocene Eocene		12,000,000 to 65,000,000
MESOZOIC Age of Reptiles	Cretaceous Jurassic Triassic		65,000,000 to 248,000,000
PALEOZOIC Age of Invertebrates, Fishes, Amphibians	Permian Carboniferous Devonian Silurian Ordovician Cambrian		248,000,000 to 590,000,000
AZOIC Primitive life	Pre-Cambrian		590,000,000 to 1,800,000,000

And this is the fact:

HUMAN REMAINS

Era	Remains	Location
Pleistocene	Skull	Olmo, Italy
	Skeleton	Clichy, France
	Skeleton	Gally Hill, England
	Pelvis	Natchez, North America
	Jaw	Abbeville, Africa
	Upper arm bone	Kanapoi, Africa
Pliocene	Skull	Calaveras, California
	Skull	Castenedolo, Italy
	Skull	Table Mt., California
	Jaw	Foxhall, England
	Footprints	Laetolil, Africa
	Footprints	Tulsa, Oklahoma
	Sandal prints	Carson City, Nevada
Miocene	Skull	Stanford, California
	Jaw	Tuscany, Italy
	Shoe print	Gobi Desert, Asia
Eocene	Skull	Germany
	Tooth	Bear Creek, Montana
Paleocene	Cast iron cube	Wolfsegg, Austria
Cretaceous	Skeletons (2)	La Sal, Utah
	Skull	Gilman, Colorado
	Tooth; footprints	Glen Rose, Texas
	Foot, shoe prints	Carrizo Valley, Oklahoma
	Cast metal nodules	Saint-Jean de Liver, France
Jurassic	Leg & foot bones	Spring Valley, Nevada
	Footprint	Parkersburg, W. Virginia
Triassic	Sandal footprint	Pershing County, Nevada
	Footprint	Mt. Victoria, Australia
Permian	Footprints	St. Louis, Missouri
Carboniferous	Footprints	Bera, Kentucky
	Iron pot	Oklahoma
	Tools	Aixen-Provence, France
	Gold chain	Illinois
	Footprints	Missouri
	Hieroglyphics	Hammondsville, Ohio
	Inscription	Philadelphia, Pennsylvania
	Imprinted slab	Webster City, Iowa
	Concrete wall	Heavener, Oklahoma
Devonian	Precision pattern	Pittsburgh, Pa.
Silurian	Skeleton	Franklin County, Mo.
Ordovician	Sandal print	Lake Windermere, England
	Metal Hammer	London, Texas
Cambrian	Sandal, footprints	Antelope Springs, Utah
	Iron bands	Lochmaree, Scotland

WHY DO WE SELDOM HEAR SUCH FACTS?

You may be asking, if such extraordinary human relics do exist, then why haven't I heard about them before?

The truth is, these facts have indeed been well documented, but have since been ignored or forgotten.

In far too many cases, the objects themselves have been mislaid, inadvertently tossed away, or sent to some museum and stored out of sight and forgotten.

Nevertheless, these discoveries are a matter of record. There are several hundred discovery reports like those in this chapter. *Scientific American* is full of them.

WHY IS THIS NOT TAUGHT IN THE SCHOOLS?

You won't hear these things in school. Shattered myths still dominate the textbooks we learn from.

Do you know that up to 200 years after the flat earth theory was disproved, schools in Europe were still teaching it as fact? Entrenched theories do die hard. It takes time.

However, a hopeful trend is emerging.

On December 1, 2003, a seminar in London, with the theme "Creationism: Science Versus Faith in Schools", was organised by *The Guardian* newspaper (UK). The function of the one day seminar was "for secondary school teachers, scientists and philosophers examining the impact of reationism on science education in a multi-faith society."

Biology tutor Sue Addinell (Islington 6th Form College) reported the changing nature of the biology syllabus. In the 1990s there had been a shift away from the evidence for evolution towards the practical application of biological science. One current textbook now had no mention of Darwin in its index.

She also noticed a change in attitudes among her pupils. In the 1970s most accepted evolution uncritically, in the 1990s there was a minority questioning it, and she now had 36 pupils - some Christians, some Muslims - but only two believed in evolution! Addinell said we must acknowledge the different views in the science classroom - to ignore them is not an option.

It is no wonder that leading evolutionists such as Steve Jones and Richard Dawkins are becoming so incensed. They are losing and they can't understand it.

Andrew Jacobs reported in the *New York Times* of January 30, 2004 that "Education officials in the [American] state of Georgia removed the word "evolution" and scaled back ideas about the natural selection of species in a proposed set of guidelines for school science classes."

That's a start!

SO WHY DOES THE SCIENTIFIC WORLD STILL HOLD TO EVOLUTION?

Many honest scientists are caught up in the system – and sincerely misinformed. It was all they were taught. They do not know about the evidence against it.

Constant exposure to something, in most cases, leads to its acceptance. As Hitler acknowledged, "Tell a lie long enough and people will come to believe it."

However, we do need to face this fact. The present system is in the grip of powerful men with enormous money behind them – and an agenda.

Established systems of science, education and public media are thoroughly committed to the belief that macro-evolution is a "fact", so you will seldom hear the FACTS about discoveries which totally upset that belief.

Carl Sagan clones repeatedly spout off words such as "billions and billions of years". And ten years of evolution is crammed down the throats of our children. By and large the Establishment refuses to accept the fossil evidence at face value.

Most university graduates have acquired their degrees through this system. They now find their careers, their reputations and their very livelihood at risk, should they admit publicly that what they have been teaching is a big mistake.

Many who have renounced the theory of evolution have not only lost funding for their projects, they have also been misrepresented, ridiculed and fired. And much of their research has then been destroyed. Examples of such treatment could fill volumes.

And here's something else to consider. It is almost impossible for any person who has taken a public stance on a certain position, to make a public admission that what he has taught is wrong.

So the unsuspecting public continues to be fed this planned menu. Those in charge influence the education system, the media and the publishing industry.

And this brings us to the big question…

IS MAN OLDER THAN EVOLUTION SAYS… OR ARE DINOSAURS AND COAL MUCH YOUNGER?

Okay, we have evidence of humans and dinosaurs together – and mankind as old as coal. So it boils down to these two alternatives:
1. Either man, the final art-piece of evolution, was on earth before the "dinosaur and coal ages" (65 to 300 million years ago),
2. Or dinosaurs and coal were not around 65 to 300 million years ago, but very recently. That is, the age of dinosaurs was the same as the "recent" age of man.

Either way, the evolution theory is in trouble.

Now, while many good folk are now coming to question the evolution fairytale, they still go for the first option – believing that man-made tools found in coal are, say, 120 million years old. They conclude that artefacts found in coal prove that man is older than the evolution theory says.

Now this may come as a shock to you, but the methods used for dating coal, dinosaurs, and so on, are just as flawed as the evolution fantasy!

This dating is part of the same evolution theory.

Now, you'll want evidence for this. Certainly, I don't ask you to take my word for it. Two chapters of evidence were provided in T*he Killing of Paradise Planet*, and I shall reveal more in the next book of this series, *The Corpse Came Back.*

But would you like to know the main, underlying reason why the evidence is rejected?

Well, like it or not, that word 'God' comes into it. That's the bottom line regarding the evolution theory.

Believe it. This is a battle between two "religions".

Did it ever occur to you that evolution theory is really a religion? Let me explain.

When Darwin offered his "Origin of Species" theory, many gladly embraced it as an alternative to "God." They wanted God out! Out of their lives, out of their memories. A hypocritical Church had turned them off. Darwin's evolution theory gave them an "out."

Evolution makes definite statements about God. It states that we have destiny in our own hands, that God plays no part in the processes around us; that we shall never answer to any God. Evolution is an atheistic religious belief – a religion and a philosophy.

As one evolutionary scientist puts it:

"In fact, evolution became in a sense a scientific religion; almost all scientists have accepted it *and many are prepared to 'bend' their observations to fit* in with it."[16]

The major issues at stake are at long last being clarified by evolutionists themselves – the DELIBERATE CHOICE of not wanting to invoke the Creator.

Dr. Michael Walker, Senior Lecturer in Anthropology, Sydney University, has said:

"One is forced to conclude that many scientists and technologists pay lip-service to Darwinian theory only because it supposedly excludes a Creator."[17]

You see, evolution is not "just another" scientific theory. Evolution is really a faith and heart commitment, a complete world-and-life view; in other words, a religion.

Evolutionary scientists dismiss the Great Flood for religious reasons… and not on objective reasons based on geological or ancient historical data.

Often, their furious rejection of any theories involving the supernatural seems almost pathological.

We take it for granted that the scientific Establishment is run by men who are all clean and honest. Jenny, wake up. Face the truth! You have no idea of the depth of corruption at the top, nor of the extreme measures taken to block the truth. Or how many scientists are fired when they renounce evolution. It is not surprising that evidence is frequently destroyed.

An embarrassing discovery

Reportedly, coal miners in West Virginia were working over one mile below the surface when they broke through a seam into an air pocket. (This had once been a water pocket.)

What they saw horrified them. Here, in coalified form, were human bodies; not just skeletons, these were bodies with noses, fingers, everything. They were on the floor, in the sides, and in the ceiling of the air pocket.

Immediately the area became a place of restricted access. Authorities rescinded the permit of the mining company to operate there.

The spot was then permanently flooded and filled with silt. Soon a dam was built over that very piece of ground and the locality has become a reservoir. How convenient!

Who gave directions to cover up this discovery? What is so threatening about the concept of catastrophe?

How deep is the swamp of lies, cover-ups and deceit in the scientific world?

In case you didn't know, a great number of highly qualified scientists have completely rejected the evolution theory. By a conservative estimate, in the United States alone, this amounts to tens of thousands.

In fact, an article in *Newsweek* in 1988 claimed that 40 percent of American scientists now believe in a God they can pray to. In every country, more and more scientists daily are opting for the Creation-and-Flood record. (Which allows for other lesser catastrophes since the Flood.)

THE FLOOD PROVIDES BETTER ANSWERS

If the global Flood really occurred, there should be:
1. Thousands of feet of water-deposited sedimentary rock layers covering most of the planet
2. Evidence that many creatures have become suddenly extinct from the event
3. Buried remains of all manner of life forms found mixed up in the sedimentary layers
4. The discovery of human remains (artefacts, footprints and skeletons) at many different depths in the Flood-produced rocks.

And this is precisely what IS found!

The fossil evidence does NOT prove gradual, nor punctuated, bursts of evolution up to man.

If a Great Flood buried all life in one enormous disaster, THEN THE EVIDENCE FITS. Most stratified rock is the result of debris laid down by water during the Great Flood. None of this strata is millions of years old. Most of these earth layers were laid down, along with human remains, during the Flood.

I said, most. Some remains which have been attributed to the Great Flood, are, rather, evidence of significant but lesser catastrophes since the Flood. In the third book of this trilogy, *The Corpse Came Back*, some of these events are covered.

I suspect that the finds at the Glen Rose site are from one such post-Flood catastrophe.

The point of this chapter is, however, that man, dinosaurs, trilobites and what have you, coexisted and died together.

* * * * * * *

Now, we all know that a chain is only as strong as its weakest link.

But, what if most of the links to complete the chain, don't exist? Suppose there virtually no links? How strong is that chain then? Let's see...

HUMAN RELICS - Summary

FOUND WHERE THEY SHOULD NOT BE
Human remains are constantly discovered mingled with or lying beneath "prehistoric" animals, or embedded in coal. This is a riddle for which the theory of evolution has no answer.

ARTIFACTS
Artifacts have been found up to 10,000 feet below the ground, and in all types of supposedly "ancient" strata.

FOOTPRINTS
Human footprints are found in undisturbed strata up to "450 million" years old.

SKELETONS
More direct is the discovery of actual human skeletons in coal seams. Such discoveries are a matter of record.

EVOLUTION THEORY WRONG
If man existed as far back as the earliest life forms, then the whole system of evolutionary theory is completely wrong.

Evolutionary geologists say the rocks are tens, even hundreds of millions of years old. Historians say that human relics in these rocks cannot be as old as that.

These "out of place" bodies indicate that dinosaurs, trilobites and humans – as well as coal beds – were buried more or less at the same time, and not millions of years apart. The exaggerated time element must be rejected.

A GLOBAL FLOOD FITS THE EVIDENCE BETTER
There is an explanation that fits the evidence much better. Most stratified rock is the result of debris laid down by water during the Great Flood, at which time most artefacts, footprints and human remains were buried.

14

The fossil gaps -
THE CASE OF THE MISSING BODIES

"I'll be back an hour before sundown," called Charles. "Going off to see the wildlife."

He waved to the oarsmen and turned to walk up the beach.

When Charles Darwin, sailing in the "Beagle", came to the Galapagos Islands, he was surprised to find on separate islands, finches that were different in size, plumage and beak shape – although they had descended from a common ancestor.

From this observed fact, Darwin's imagination took a giant leap. "Perhaps," he fantasised, "humans and even grass came from the same original mother."

Yeah, sure they did.

* * * * * * *

From Darwin's theory, an evolution time chart was sketched. The story went that a simple cell may have gradually evolved into more complex forms and finally into man!

I remember sitting in school one day and hearing my teacher say:

"The first forms of life were small creatures of simple organization. After long ages of time, these became more complex forms, and later became still higher, until finally appeared present animals, plants and man.

"All this is so certain that geologists can tell how old a rock is, by the kind of fossils it contains.

"The deeper rock layers (with simpler fossils) were laid down first. Over long ages, the other layers were deposited on top, containing increasingly complex organisms.

"See this chart on the wall? It illustrates the geological history of the world." (The chart from which she taught us is reproduced in Chapter 13.)

FOSSILS ARE FOUND IN ROCK STRATA
On top of the earth's crust, at the surface, are usually great thicknesses of water-laid sediments which have solidified into rock. These lie one upon another much like layers of a cake. Often they contain remains or casts of animals and plants which once lived.
The deeper strata usually contain simpler fossils than the shallower rocks. But there are many exceptions to this rule.

THE "EARLIEST" FOSSILS
Having learned science at school, I started digging into this fascinating subject some more.
What my teacher had told me sounded more or less plausible. But as an inquisitive, but careful researcher, I was soon to face a few shocks.

A. *The first complex sea life had "no ancestors".*
You'll notice in the evolution chart on page 139 that near the bottom of the strata is the age called 'CAMBRIAN". This comprises layers of rock loaded with small sea creatures – molluscs, jellyfish, worms and trilobites – in their thousands.
Scientists have spent much time searching below this in the "older" PRE-CAMBRIAN strata for the **ancestors** of these creatures. These Pre-Cambrian sediments (often 5,000 feet deep) were suitable for the preservation of fossils because they are often identical with the overlaying rocks which contain fossils, yet no fossils are found in them.
The result has been a virtual blank.
So the forerunners of the complexly organised sea creatures are nowhere to be found.
There is NO EVIDENCE of slow and sporadic appearance.

B. *They appeared suddenly, already perfect.*
In these earliest Cambrian rocks, "all of the important invertebrate phyla are already represented."[1]
Even the "simplest" of these organisms show "extreme complexity".[2]
The evidence shows that they came "into existence suddenly and in FULL perfection."[3]

As I surveyed the evidence worldwide, this one fact kept cropping up: Every fossil species, when it first appears in the rocks, is **already complete** and fully organised. There is no evidence that any "half and half" form ever existed.

From all appearance, based on **known fossil evidence**, there occurred a sudden great outburst of life at a high level of complexity.

This discovery was in clear contradiction to the evolutionary theory I had been taught at school.

As another scientist observes:

"New groups of plants and animals suddenly appear, apparently without any close ancestors... Most major groups appear this way... The fossil record which has produced the problem is not much help in its solution... Some palaeontologists believe that these events tell a story not in accord with the theory."[4]

SUBSEQUENT FOSSIL "PERIODS"

So much for the "earliest" forms of life. But what of the subsequent "ages"?

Darwin hoped that eventually evidence would be found in the fossils entombed "progressively" in the earth's strata.[5]

"If evolution has taken place, there will its marks be found; if it has not taken place, there will be its refutation."[6]

If, for example, reptiles gradually evolved into birds, we should find remains of reptiles becoming progressively more bird-like, until they are fully bird. Such transitional series of fossils should link all categories of life. There should be no systematic gaps.

So what is found?

NO CONNECTING LINKS
BETWEEN FOSSIL GROUPS

These hoped-for links are still non-existent. Says a disappointed evolutionist: "A century of digging since Darwin's time has only made their absence more glaring... Palaeontologists have devoted whole careers to looking for examples of gradual transitions over time, and with a few exceptions THEY HAVE FAILED."[7]

"Despite the bright promise that paleontology provides a means of "seeing" evolution, it has presented some nasty difficulties for evolutionists, the most notorious of which is the presence of "gaps" in the fossil record. **Evolution requires intermediate forms between species and paleontology does not provide them...**"[8]

"Contrary to what most scientists write, **the fossil record does not support the Darwinian theory of evolution** because it is this theory (there are several) which we use to interpret the fossil record. By doing so, we are guilty of **circular reasoning** if we then say the fossil record supports this theory."[9]

There are **"no transitional fossils,"** writes Dr. Colin Patterson, Senior Palaeontologist at the British Museum of Natural History. "I will lay it on the line – there is not one such fossil for which one could make a watertight argument."[10]

Professor Gould of Harvard University admits the same:

"All paleontologists know... transitions between major groups are characteristically abrupt."[11]

The evolution theory predicted that there would be found countless **intermediary stages** between all forms of life – but there are none, either in nature today or in the fossil record of the past.

The same theory states that once upon a time a reptile turned into... A BIRD!

The naivety of that statement is so breathtaking, I need a glass of water.

For one thing, a reptile and a bird are built on a **different basic design**. Evolution would have to totally scrap the reptile design – and RE-DESIGN from the start.

How could we have ever believed that heavy-boned reptiles, with scales, could change into light, efficient "flying machines" with feathers, wings, bird feet, beaks and songs – as well as endless other unique characteristics?

Our now abundant fossil inventory does not contain even one fossil partially covered with feathers and partially with scales.

And take bats. From what animal did bats evolve? From mice, some theorists tell us. But where are the intermediary forms? There are NONE in fossil form, nor are there any in existence today. It is a HUGE jump from mice's feet to bat's wings, and from ordinary ears and nostrils to the intricate sonar system possessed by bats.

In any case, as an honest evolutionist says, "the fossil evidence does not bear out the supposition."[12]

Austin H. Clark, of the Smithsonian Institution, Washington, notes:

> "The whale line is always distinct from every other line of mammalian development... Just as whales were always whales, seals were always seals... Among the more familiar mammals, the cat and dog lines are always separate. No forms intermediate between cats and their relatives and dogs and their relatives are known."[13]

Chester A. Arnold, Professor of Botany and Curator of Fossil Plants, University of Michigan, says concerning fossil plants:

> "As yet we have not been able to trace the phylogenetic history of a single group of modern plants from the beginning to the present."[14]

Even worse is the statement of E.J.H. Corner, Professor of Tropical Botany at Cambridge University. He wrote:

> "I still think that, to the unprejudiced, the fossil record of plants is in favour of special creation."[15]

Is it really THAT bad?

Let Heribert-Nilsson, an outstanding scientist, at one time Director of the Botanical Institute in Lund, Sweden, answer:

> "The true situation is that those fossils have not been found which were expected... it has been impossible to find the connecting types."[16]

Another noted evolutionary authority concedes:

> "The fossil record nevertheless continues to be composed mainly of gaps."[17]

In fact, 90% of the "expected" fossil record is not there. The only part that does exist corresponds (in general terms) with the living creatures of today (except for those fossil types which are extinct – and extinction is not evolution).

The missing 90% comprises the intermediate "links" that the evolution theory predicts – but which have never been found in the fossil record, nor in today's living world.

In short, the fossils provide no evidence of evolution.

Those fossils that are found are fully formed and perfect – with no lead-ups to them.

Just what you'd expect if they'd been specially created.

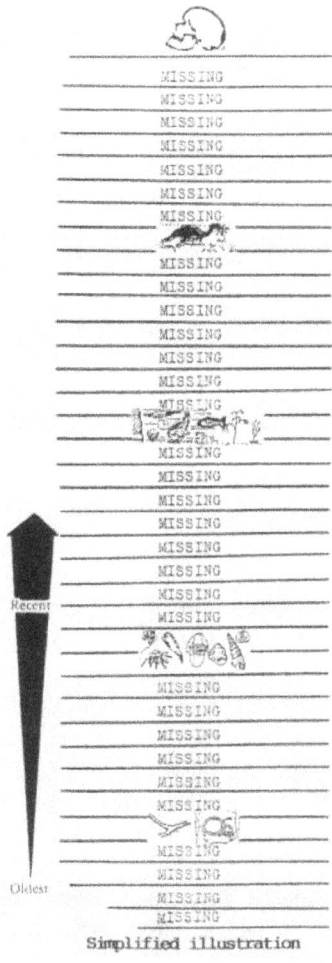

The fossil record is composed mainly of gaps.

Some scientists recognise this, but admit that the thought is unpalatable.

Are the links still awaiting discovery?
So they put forward the idea that the fossil record does not show evolution, simply because the missing links are still to be found.

I should let Dr. Norman D. Newell of Columbia University respond to that idea:
> "Experience shows that gaps which separate the highest categories may never be bridged in the fossil record. Many of the discontinuities tend to be more and more emphasised with increased collecting."[18]

Dr. David M. Raup, Curator of Geology, Field Museum of Natural History, Chicago, also says:
> "Well, we are now about 120 years after Darwin and the knowledge of the fossil record has been greatly expanded. We now have a quarter of a million fossil species but the situation hasn't changed much. The record of evolution is still surprisingly jerky and, ironically, we have even fewer examples of evolutionary transition than we had in Darwin's time."[19]

Some supposed links

Now I can just hear someone asking, What about the platypus? Isn't that a link between reptiles and mammals? And the archaeopteryx? That resembles both birds and reptiles.

Here is what Dr. Richard M. Ritland of Harvard University says:
> "Occasionally we find fossils of extinct life forms whose place is between widely separated present-day groups. 'Archaeopteryx,' for instance, is a little-known type of fossil resembling both birds and reptiles. But this may represent another group, distinct from both types. In the fossil record, the higher categories remain separate from the time they first appeared."[20]

And here's the crunch: every crucial feature of Archaeopteryx is perfectly formed – no half-legs, half-wings or half-scale feathers, etcetera.

Alan Feduccia of the University of North Carolina has found that crucial evidence has been overlooked in the rush to claim Archaeopteryx as transitional.

It's wings have the same aerodynamic shape used by birds today to achieve lift, and the hind claws are identical to those of modern perching birds. He concludes it is definitely not a running, feathered dinosaur. It is "not a transitional form but a fully-fledged bird".[21]

"Paleontologists have tried to turn Archaeopteryx into an earth-bound, feathered dinosaur," says Feduccia. "But it's not. It is a bird, a perching bird. And no amount of 'paleobabble' is going to change that."

Are there any transitional forms anywhere? Dr. Colin Patterson, Senior Paleontologist at the British Museum of Natural History, in London, said this in the personal letter quoted earlier in this chapter:

"... I fully agree with your comments on the **lack of** direct illustration of **evolutionary transitions** in my book. If I knew of any, fossil or living, I would certainly have included them... Yet Gould and the American Museum people are hard to contradict when they say there are **no transitional fossils**... I will lay it on the line – there is not one such fossil for which one could make a watertight argument."

Sudden "leaps" in evolution?

To account for this embarrassing lack of fossil evidence in the rocks for evolution, the following idea has surfaced nowadays. It is called "punctuated equilibrium".

Perhaps, goes the suggestion, the major evolutionary changes occurred quite rapidly, while the population levels were low. So the gaps may be due to such periods of 'explosive evolution', which occurred so rapidly they left no trace in the fossils.

In other words, very fast evolutionary development occurred in small isolated communities that was NOT recorded in the fossil strata.

Of course, there is no physical evidence for this theory. It is an argument from silence and is therefore a position of faith.

I feel sorry for the "new evolutionist", but that will not do. A theory which predicts it will have no evidence hardly qualifies as a scientific theory.

Those who promote this theory do admit that the theory hasn't got a mechanism. To date they have not been able to point to any experiment which will confirm that evolutionary jumps have a means by which they can occur!

Let's be honest about this. Such a theory is **not scientific observation**. We are asked to believe that evolution occurs so slowly today that we cannot detect it, and so rapidly in the past (in the fossil world) that we cannot detect it!

But, did you know, there is observed evidence that actually refutes this idea.

In *Science News*, 28 June 1986, p.410, the AIDS virus was shown to mutate up to a million times faster than the DNA for other organisms.

In this case, we have an example of what would actually happen if very fast development DID occur in a small isolated community as some suggest. In one year then, the virus went through the equivalent of 1 million years of mutation at the usual rate. But even with the mutation process speeded up a million times, the AIDS virus only 'evolved' into another form of AIDS virus and nothing else.

This is the same story as the fossils tell us. The first spiders mutated and selected into the forms we have today. They remain spiders. The behaviour of the AIDS virus and the testimony of the rock record therefore largely refute the theory of "punctuated equilibrium" as a means of evolution.

THE IMPASSIBLE CHASMS

Fred John Meldau draws attention to:
* An impassible gulf between inorganic matter and the amazingly intricate viruses.
* An impassible gulf between viruses and bacteria.
* An impassible gulf between bacteria and the somatic cell (the basis of all life).

* An impassible gulf between protozoa (e.g. amoeba) that multiply by simple cell division, and the higher forms of life that multiply by sex.
* An impassible gulf between all animal phyla and all plant divisions.
* Impossible gulfs between all classes.
* Impossible gulfs between all orders.
* Impossible gulfs between all families.
* Impossible gulfs between all genera.
* Impossible gulfs between all different species of protozoa.[22]

So what does that leave us with? CHASMS, GULFS and GAPS ... UNBRIDGEABLE GAPS!

Evolution must be accepted on **faith alone**, since nine-tenths of the record is missing – with gaps that are, it seems, unbridgeable. British zoologist G.A. Kerket put it this way: "The evidence for what did happen is not available."[23]

It is important to bear this in mind: the absence of evidence is **not evidence** of absence!

I put it to you that after 145 years since Darwin the evidence **IS** in. But it is not what the evolutionist had expected.

Dr. Norman D. Newell of Columbia University says: "Experience shows that gaps which separate the highest categories **may never be bridged** in the fossil record. Many of the discontinuities tend to be more and more emphasised with increased collecting."[24]

Paleontologist David Kitts adds: "Evolution requires intermediate forms between species and paleontology does not provide them"[25]

The chain needed links and the links are not there. As we said, a chain is only as strong as its WEAKEST link. How strong, then, is a chain with NO links? You tell me.

EVOLUTION, THEREFORE, UNPROVEN

Remember what Darwin's champion, T.H. Huxley said: "If evolution has taken place, there [in the fossils] will its marks be found; if it has not taken place, there will be its refutation."[26]

And more recently, Niles Eldridge, curator of New York's Natural History Museum, admitted: "The fossil record we were told to find in the past 120 years [since Darwin] does not exist."[27]

And if the **fossils** do not give evidence of evolution, there remains no evidence that life has evolved, at all.

On the contrary, the fossil record shows the very situation which the Genesis account of Creation indicates – fixity within basic types and no inter-connecting forms of animal or plant between those types. To be true, it does not **prove** creation, but the evidence is **consistent** with it.

The intergrading forms necessary to indicate evolution are notably absent.

D. Dwight Davis, Curator, Division of Vertebrate Anatomy, Chicago Natural History Museum, in discussing the problems of these gaps, was honest enough to admit:

> "But the facts of paleontology confirm equally well with other interpretations...., e.g., divine creation.... And paleontology by itself can neither prove nor refute such ideas."[28]

If evolution is true:	If creation is true:
The fossil record should show transitional series linking all categories of life. There should be no systematic gaps between them.	The fossil record should show the sudden appearance of each created type with ordinal characteristics complete. Sharp boundaries should separate major taxonomic groups.

You draw your own conclusions as to which scenario fits the fossil evidence.

On this point the statement of two University of California scientists is rather interesting:

> "The abrupt appearance of higher taxa in the fossil record has been a perennial puzzle.... Not only do characteristic and distinctive remains of phyla appear suddenly, without known ancestors, but several classes of a phylum, orders of a class, and so on, commonly appear at approximately the same time, without known intermediates."[29]

Fossils prove evolution? Of course not.

* * * * * * *

And now, jump into the boat with me and visit the Forbidden Islands! Are you ready? Let's go...

15

Living fossils -
SORRY, NO CHANGE

Just a short distance from our home, some ten miles off shore, is a quaint cluster of pinnacles jutting out from the Pacific Ocean.

Would you believe, these Aldermen Islands were named as a joke.

In 1769, the famous British navigator James Cook was sailing along the New Zealand coast. After discovering (and naming) Mayor Island, on the London Lord Mayor's birthday, Cook's vessel came next upon these freakish-looking isles.

And what an odd conglomeration! Some tall, others squat, paunchy or bald. No wonder the amused crew went overboard (so to speak) in matching each one with a different member of that mayor's distinguished council – the London aldermen!

There is good reason why government decree forbids any landing by visitors on the Aldermen Islands. These islands constitute one of the last remaining haunts of New Zealand's "living fossil", the 2 foot long lizard-like tuatara.

But it is feared that just one innocent disruption could result in the loss of a whole generation. Tuatara eggs require 15 months to hatch and the young take 20 years to mature.

These "fossils" are alive! And I shall tell you more about the tuatara in a minute.

The tuatara and some other animals believed to have been extinct for aeons and which **therefore have been used to date the strata in which they were found as fossils,** have since been discovered very much alive.

"EARLIEST" FORMS STILL ALIVE

So-called "earliest" creatures are still with us.

- The Coelacanth, a fish with "legs", supposedly lived 75 million years ago. It was long believed to be an extinct ancestor of land animals – until it was discovered alive and well in the Indian Ocean.

Fossils of this fish had been found in rocks "75 million years old", but in no rocks since "that time." But then they appear alive again now! How shall we explain that? Perhaps those 75 million years are only imagination?

- As I mentioned above, living only on some islands off the coast of New Zealand is a reptile called the tuatara. Its so-called third eye is a mechanism sensitive to light, under the skin of the forehead.

Fossils of these creatures are found in Europe and Asia, in rocks which are theoretically 135 million years old.

But none exist in the strata allegedly laid down since then. Yet, after this supposed absence of 135 million years, we suddenly find them alive in the modern world – and unchanged from their original fossil form.

That's right. During all that time, the tuatara has stayed the same; it has not evolved at all!

Now, if it had **really** been living on earth for the past 135 million years, shouldn't its fossils be in rocks spanning these 135 million years?

But they are not!

MANY OF THEM

There are hundreds of other "living fossils" which pose the same dilemma. Could it be that those hundreds of millions of years never existed?

MODERN DESCENDANTS UNCHANGED

And the surprises keep coming. Modern, living descendants of fossil organisms are essentially unchanged. The coelacanth fish – no evolution in 75 million years! The tuatara – no evolution in 135 million years! The common ant – precisely the same, even to its peculiar habits, still the same after "millions" of years.

And you can say that for virtually every type of creature.

Guess what. When the first spiders appear in the Palaeozoic, they do so abruptly. They look just like the spiders we have today. They are made of the same spiders' cuticle, and are equipped with spinnerets – the organs they use to spin thread. In fact, microscopic examination reveals that their legs had tarsal claws used for weaving webs, just as web-weaving types do now.

The same is true of plants. Kauri pine fossils found in Mesozoic strata are the same as Kauri pines today.[1]

The living cycads that we have today are unchanged from their first appearance in the Mesozoic. The Ginkgo tree preserved in the rock record is virtually indistinguishable from the specimens in our gardens. Among the first flowering plants recorded in the Mesozoic are Magnolias. They are unchanged today. Bats which appear in Cenozoic rocks are fully developed and have only minor variations from today's forms.

Listen to A.H. Clark, an authority on marine fossils:

"One of the most striking and important facts which have been established through a study of the fossil animals is that from the very earliest times, **from the very first beginnings** of the fossil record, the broader aspects of the animal life upon the earth **have remained unchanged**.

"…. Throughout the fossil record these major groups have remained essentially unchanged. This means that the **interrelationships** between them likewise have remained unchanged."[2]

Did you get that? The fossils comprise exactly the same groups that live today. (Of course, some animals have become extinct, but extinction is not evolution.)

And the same gaps exist. Do you realise what that means?

If the separation of the main divisions of nature was just the same in the past as it is today - if, for example, ancient birds and ancient reptiles were as separate from each other as their present-day descendants are - then I'm sorry, the whole concept of evolution collapses.

Let's ponder that just once more. There is evidence of NO EVOLUTIONARY PROGRESSION. The only fossils found from the past are those that correspond in general terms to those living now (plus some extinct types – but extinction is not evolution).

German biologist and paleontologist Dr. Joachim Scheven has amassed a collection of transparencies which show more than **500 examples** in his personal possession of living creatures **virtually identical** to fossil forms.

The overwhelming message of the fossil record is one of **staying the same** - not evolving. Of course, many types have gone extinct. Those also show no sign of real evolution throughout their former existence.

**Variation within clear boundaries,
but no new basic types**

Because you and I were not there at the start, we can only theorise from the evidence. A theory that takes into account **all** the available **evidence**, would go something like this:

All the basic kinds of flora and fauna were present initially. The representative of each kind began with **a larger gene pool originally**, that divided by migration and selection to give variations within each kind.

Through catastrophe, a significant number of the original kinds have become extinct.

Changed conditions after catastrophe allowed some remaining types to become predominant.

This makes great variation possible

Such a theory allows for immense variation within the kind or species. Natural selection will occur, but only if the information for the change is already in the gene pool. In the case of dogs, for example, this approach suggests that an original ancestor probably gave rise to wolves, foxes, coyotes, hyenas, jackals and the original 'mongrel' dog called 'Tomarctus'. From the large gene pool of Tomarctus, all 110 or more forms of dog have been bred.

Each variety loses original genetic information

In breeding out long-haired forms such as a Samoyed or Husky, there is a loss of genetic information that would give rise to short-haired forms, and so on. Selection, whether by natural processes or manipulated by mankind, always results in this genetic information loss in flora and fauna. Highly bred dogs therefore contain less genetic information than a mongrel. The gene pool has been divided by the selection process. Note further that these varieties are still plainly and obviously dogs. The boundary of the dog kind has certainly not been usurped.

Does species "break up" produce a new species?

You may be wondering, what about those varieties of life-form that used to interbreed, but no longer do? Doesn't this mean they have become a separate species? So doesn't that prove gene-pool expansion?

Let's stick to observational fact. As each kind spreads abroad, it tends to 'break-up' into different varieties, as did the dog kind. Another well-known example concerns varieties of flies. It matters little whether this break-up occurs 'naturally' or is induced by humans.

Nevertheless, when this break-up has occurred, even varieties that no longer inter-breed can be recognised as descendants of the same original kind, as they only possess alternate forms (or 'alleles') of the same genes.

Furthermore, each variety now contains a smaller gene-pool than the original ancestor. This implies restricted abilities to cope with changing conditions, which is what extinction is all about.

Creatures changing today:
Isn't that evolution?

I hear someone ask, But what about the many varieties of creatures that keep changing today. Isn't that evolution?

Good question.

Well, the laws of genetics show that each basic type, whether dog, butterfly, or human, has programmed into it the capacity for variation. This ensures survival in different environments. But the organism's DNA programme (inbuilt set of instructions) imposes limits:
* variations within the "kind", yes.
* capacity to turn into a different type of organism, no!

Variation within the same type – yes. Re-design to become another type of creature – no.

There is tremendous potential for varieties within a single type of animal or plant. The more grotesque the characteristic, the weaker and less viable the offspring become. Cross-breeding tends to return them to their original form.

Here is another example. From the wild rock pigeon, *Columbia Livia*, over 300 domesticated breeds of pigeon have been developed. Their diversity of form and temperament are so astounding that different 'species' or even 'generic' names would have been assigned if it had not been known that they all had a common ancestor.[3]

Here is actual proof of the huge potential for variation within one created basic type through obvious gene-pool division via selection. It also points out the practical difficulty of labelling different species. This suggests that the number of true species may be less than anticipated. Finally, the boundary of the basic type has again not been transgressed: they are still very obviously, and beautifully, pigeons!

What this means

So what is the observational evidence? That only 'sub-speciation' occurs – that is, variation within the basic type.

Change from one basic type, to another, has never been witnessed.

We cannot extrapolate and say that, because variation within a kind is seen, then a leap from one kind to another must also have taken place. This would be logically fallacious, since it is unsupported by experimentation – and it is likewise unsupported by the fossil evidence.

The fact is: *"Loss, not gain, of genetic information".*
1. Selection divides the gene pool.
2. Mutations are nearly always harmful, with genetic information becoming garbled or lost.

For a one-celled organism to change into a more complex one, vast amounts of functionally useful information would need to be progressively added to the genetic code.

However, the examples most folk think of as evolution (such as natural selection favoring DDT-resistant mosquitoes) are doing precisely the opposite – losses, not gains of information. Mutations are unable to add such information. Overall, they degrade genetic information.

The most viable theory, therefore, is gene pool division and extinction.

Interestingly, the book of Genesis accords with modern scientific observation: that after the creation of all floral and fauna kinds, they were programmed to "reproduce after their kind" (as seen in the fossil evidence), and not to change from one kind into another as the theory of gene pool expansion requires for evolution.

So what is the bottom line? What is consistent with the evidence? Simply this: All kinds of life-forms were present originally. Each catastrophe since has resulted in some extinctions. And the changed conditions allowed some remaining types to dominate.

TO SUMMARISE

In this and the preceding chapter, we have discovered that the remains of past life forms on this planet – the "fossils" – pose at least four problems for the evolution theory:

1. Complex fossils appear in the *"earliest"* strata, with *no evidence of ancestors.*
2. Each plant and animal type appears abruptly in the *subsequent* fossil record, with *no evidence of any transitional form.* It comes as an *already complete,* functional unit.
3. There are persistent, *unbridgeable gaps* or chasms *between* major types of organisms.
4. Those plant and animal varieties that survive today are basically *unchanged* from their first fossil ancestors.

The fossils show no evidence that a development from simple to complex ever took place in the history of life on earth. And the swarm of ancient creatures left *no trace* of evolutionary ancestors because THEY HAD NONE.

Still with me? Good. Now for the BIG ROCK mystery...

FOSSILS: SUDDEN; NO LINKS - Summary

1. **THE EARLIEST FOSSILS**

    Darwin predicted that past life forms would show a **gradual** change from simplest ancestral forms into more and more complex forms. Creationists, on the other hand, predicted that the fossil record should show the **sudden** appearance in great variety of highly complex forms.
    So what do the fossils show?
    * **The first complex sea life had "no ancestors".** The "earliest" fossils, instead of appearing slowly and sporadically, **suddenly** appear in their thousands in the Cambrian strata. Since Darwin's time, scientists have spent much time searching the lower, "older," Pre-Cambrian strata for evidence of ancestors to these "earliest" creatures whose remains have been found. The result? A virtual blank. So where did this oceanful of complex sea creatures come from, if the "next oldest" layer does not reveal their ancestors?
    * **They appeared suddenly, already perfect.** Every fossil species, when it first appears in the rocks, is **already complete and fully organised**. There is no evidence that any "half and half" form ever existed. From all appearance, based on known fossil evidence, there occurred a sudden great outburst of life at a high level of complexity. These facts are a clear contradiction to the evolutionary theory.

2. **SUBSEQUENT FOSSIL PERIODS**

    According to the evolutionary theory, the fossil record should show transitional series linking all categories of life. There should be no systematic gaps between them. Creationists, on the other hand, predicted that sharp boundaries should separate major taxonomic groups; each created type should appear suddenly, with no transitional forms between them.
    What, then, are the facts?

* **There are no connecting links between fossil groups.** There are "missing ages" in localities everywhere; there are thousands of missing links; more than that, there are great jumps. The fossils do not show continuing evolutionary progression at all. True connecting links are as absent between all major fossil groups as between the same living groups today. As one evolutionary authority concedes: "The fossil record... continues to be **composed mainly of gaps.**" The expected intermediate forms between types of animals **are all missing, without exception.**

The fossils pose this double problem for evolution:
1. The appearance of complex fossils in the **"earliest" strata**, with **no traceable ancestors.**
2. The **persistent gaps between** major types of organisms.

Fossils, therefore, are of no use to evolution. The supposed proofs of evolution can be more satisfactorily interpreted in terms of a simultaneous Creation, followed by the Great Flood. The obvious catastrophic manner in which the earth's sedimentary strata (with their fossils) were laid down, renders the geological timescale totally meaningless.

16

Rocks "older" at the bottom? -
DON'T TRY TO MOVE OLD BEDS

    Last summer, I carried into our garage all of those items that were not in regular use in the house. My wife Josephine likewise sorted through her things that were cluttering up space. We packed them into cartons and very soon a tall stack of boxes was reaching toward the garage ceiling.

    Probably the point I am about to make will be so obvious, it hardly needs mentioning. But humor me anyway, please.

    Let's say you walk in just as I have finished stacking the boxes. And I ask you this question: "Guess which box I put onto that pile last."

    You would cast me a look which says "Don't insult my intelligence," and then you would point to the box at the top of the pile, right?

    It's so obvious, it's silly to ask. What's on top was placed there last. The carton at the bottom was put there first.

    Now this brings me to a BIG PROBLEM in the rock layers (strata) of our planet.

    Notice the simplified diagram below. So-called "ancient" dinosaurs (which lived and were buried first) are found buried in top layers; humans (who appeared last) are found buried way down lower.

    The same goes for so-called "earliest" life forms, which are sometimes found buried in the highest, most "recent" layers of rock.

    But not always. Sometimes they are found midway up; in fact, they can be anywhere at all.

    You see the problem, don't you? If evolution theory is correct, the "oldest" ones (buried first) should be lower down. And the youngest, the "most recent", should be in the top layer.

What I'm saying is that as we examine the earth's strata, we discover that:

THESE EARTH LAYERS CONTAINING FOSSILS ARE OFTEN IN THE "WRONG" ORDER.

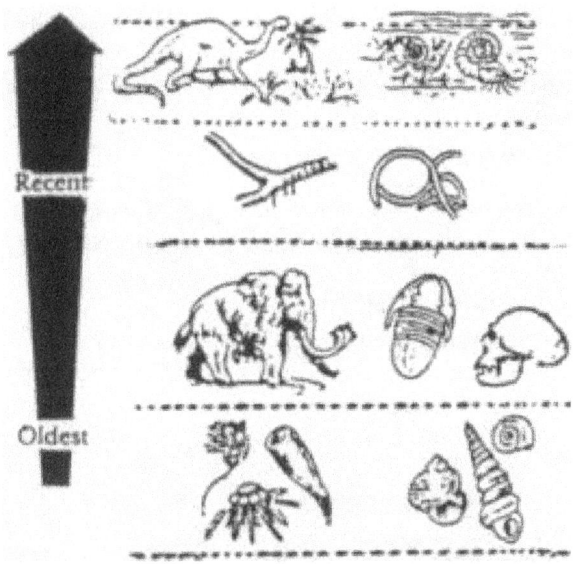

There are locations in almost every part of the world where this occurs.

In fact, such a reversed order can be found repeated two or three times in the same vertical section.

Many cases have been observed of the very "youngest" Quarternary rocks resting directly upon the "oldest", with all the intervening "ages" omitted!

Or frequently the **"oldest"** rocks are on the surface and have the physical appearance of young rocks, **soft and unconsolidated**. And "young rocks may well be as crystalline and metamorphic as the very "oldest".

Every large mountain range in the world has been found to contain these upside-down strata.
* In Glacier National Park, U.S.A., a block of Pre-Cambrian limestone "a **billion** years old" (and stretching 350 miles by 35 miles by 6 miles thick) lies ON TOP OF Cretaceous shales only (!) "100 million years old."
* In a very large area of the Rockies, extending from Alberta to Montana, Cambrian and other "old" rocks (containing "primitive" trilobite and similar fossils) lie horizontally on top of soft Cretaceous shales for 500 miles. At the same time, dinosaurs and large, complex animals are deep down underneath.)
* In the Salt Range in Pakistan, the "oldest" Cambrian beds occur on top of "more recent" Tertiary for many miles of its area.

Pardon me if I ask a silly question. But…does this mean that the "oldest" fossils are "younger" than the "youngest" ones?

Did it happen by "over-thrusting"?

So how does the evolution expert explain these?

"Oh, these old beds must have been lifted up and pushed over on top of younger beds," comes the reply.

So when we find the order of the fossils contradicting a theory, what must we do? Simple. We invent **immense** contortions of the earth's crust to save the theory.

So mountain ranges, we are told, have been pushed for many miles across soft shales WITHOUT INJURING THEM! These mountain ranges have travelled considerable distances across valleys and up over other mountains.

Now, would you please think about this. Can you see the problem?

Do not these rocks cover an IMMENSE area – and look HORIZONTAL STILL – and normal?

Here are some examples:
* Chief Mountain in Montana needs to have travelled across the plains and climbed the slope of another mountain and then settled on it.
* The Heart Mountain Thrust of Wyoming, the Bannock Overthrust of Utah, and many areas of the Rockies offer more

examples of vast areas of rocks, THOUSANDS OF FEET THICK, that "climbed up" over other areas, but left no evidence at the so-called fault line, nor anywhere else, of their incredible journeys.
* A similar upside-down "displacement" in China extends over 500 miles.
* Another in Scandinavia covers 85,000 square miles.
In fact, you'll find examples like these in every part of the world.
I would like to know, how could millions of tons of rocks laid down earlier climb on top of rocks laid down later?
How could this happen to entire mountains and valleys? - and for thousands of miles in area **remain totally smooth and even**, with **no signs of wear**, breakage or twisting?
* The Lewis Overthrust is 6 miles thick and 135 to 350 miles long. What if I told you that this object over 30,000 feet (9,000 metres) thick had to slide 35 to 40 miles to thrust over to its present location?
Now if the top of the rocks on which it now rests was at sea level and if the overthrust rested beside it, then the top of the overthrust would have had to extend 31,580 feet into the sky.
The overthrust would need to have climbed more than 2,000 feet higher than Mount Everest.
You've got to laugh, really.
But there's more. In order for it to be higher enough to slide downhill 35 to 40 miles, the overthrust had to jump still higher – so high that it is beyond the range of credibility.
The laws of dynamics and mechanics show that this rock would pulverise into dust before it could overcome the friction of being shifted across another stratum.
This overthrust should have produced at least a large mass of broken rock in front of it and along the sides. But this has not been found.
* The Mythen peak "overthrust" of the Alps is said to have made the journey all the way from Africa!
You've got to be kidding.
"What could have caused these mountains to travel across valleys and uphill with their masses of granite weighing billions of tons?" asks Velikovsky. "No force acting from inside the earth,

pulling inward or pushing outward, could have created these overthrusts."[1]

F.K. Mather of Harvard University admits: "Geologists have not yet found a satisfactory escape from this dilemma."[2]

Reginald A. Daly of Harvard concluded that geological history, for example, in North America, "holds ten major mysteries for every one that has already been solved."[3]

How frustrating this must be! There are well-documented cases of rock-dates being adjusted because "unwelcome" fossils have been found in them.

This is what goes on behind closed doors. It's the evolution theory in action!

But what do authorities on isostasy and tectonics have to say about such theories? They state that such alleged horizontal faulting is "absurd, from an engineering point of view" and "a mechanical impossibility."[4]

It is clearly only the theory of evolution that insists the **upper** beds were deposited **before the lower** beds were laid down. But I ask you, wouldn't it be simpler to assume that these natural features were deposited where they are?

This raises another problem. Geologists who subscribe to evolution hold to uniformism, the idea that "existing processes acting in the same manner and with essentially the same intensity as at present are sufficient to account for all geological changes."[5]

But, to explain the embarrassing "fossils in the wrong order" evidence, the evolution theorist is driven to insist on mountains sliding for miles in a way that could **not** happen now.

Let me say this. If the idea of a world Flood is fantastic, then the notion of mountains travelling for hundreds of miles without a known cause, must be seen as even more fantastic.

BETWEEN LAYERS:
100 MILLION YEARS MISSING

Here is something you find all over the world. The picture below is at Port Waikato in New Zealand.

The top portion of this cliff, you notice, is nicely layered. At the bottom of the cliff it's grey and messy.

Photo: Creation Research

The evolution theory regards the top layered rocks as the Miocene and the bottom rocks as Semi-metamorphose Jurassic. In the evolutionist's mind, the difference in age between the two is about 100 million years.

This example brings to light the fact that in New Zealand, as in the world at large, there is no geological column showing all so-called strata representing millions of years of evolutionary history.

If I am trying to trace my family tree through aeons of years, it matters not if there's a time gap of one million years, ten million years, or one hundred million years. Any gap means I have NO TRACEABLE FAMILY TREE.

Oh, bother!

ALL AND EVERY ROCK TYPE AT THE BOTTOM

Down near the bottom of the Grand Canyon, just above the granite, are rocks known as "Cambrian", in which are found animals such as trilobites, graptolites and brachiopods. In the early days, we are told, these were the only life-forms on earth.

But do these Cambrian rocks extend everywhere around the globe at the bottom, next to the foundation granite?

Not on your life! They are found *only here and there*.

In many places, and over wide areas, different rock categories, Carboniferous, Cretaceous or Tertiary (containing huge, complex animals) are found as bottom layers, resting directly on the granite - instead of the Cambrian.

Around the world, **EVERY SINGLE ONE of the different sets of rock "age"** is found in the **bottom position.**

This means that if the bottom rocks contain the oldest forms of life, then in one part of the world life started with the Cambrian (the simplest fossils); elsewhere it began with the Tertiary (higher forms of life); and somewhere else it began with the intermediate animals.

OR WERE ALL FORMS IN EXISTENCE AT THE SAME TIME?

Just think what this means.

But that's not all…

LIFE-FORMS FROM "DIFFERENT AGES" ARE FOUND MIXED UP IN THE SAME STRATUM

The main buttress of the evolutionary theory is the supposed fact that the fossil-bearing strata everywhere exhibit the same order. Any textbook on historical geology will make this claim. (See the geological time chart on page 139.)

However, this is definitely not so.

I'm talking about the REAL world now. Frequently fossils from different "ages" are found "mixed up" – and over thousands of square miles. (We suggested this in earlier chapters.) Strata are found in near random order.

It is safe to say that in some location or other, one could find practically *any sequence* whatever of the so-called "geological ages".

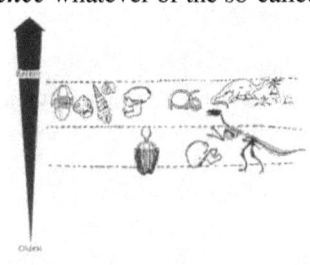

Is this telling us that the creatures of our planet **did NOT evolve one after another**, but LIVED AT THE SAME TIME?   No evolutionary sequence, Mary.

The fact that creatures from different imaginary "ages" are found mixed together, buried at the same level, can only show that:
All life forms were contemporaneous.
All forms of life have always existed together.
The evidence shows this – and there is no hard evidence against it.

The truth is that with few exceptions, the fossils furnish us with a **cross-section** of the organisms living at the time the Deluge struck. They are **not** a progressive historical Disaster.
Now here's another killer discovery…record, but a monument to all life existing and destroyed in that Great

INDIVIDUAL FOSSILS THROUGH SEVERAL "AGES" OF STRATA

* In Cragleith Quarry, England, a fossil tree was found penetrating through 12 successive layers of sedimentary limestone rock.
* Fossilised tree trunks frequently extend 30 or more feet through several layers of rock. Some extend through two or more seams of coal; each seam is interspersed with sedimentary material – which by uniformitarian theory should have taken "aeons" to form.
* In the picture on the next page, Jeff Smith, long time industrial chemist, stands beside a fossil pine tree in the Pilot coal seams south of Newcastle, Australia.

Here are at least 14 coal seams, each of them supposed to have formed slowly over thousands or millions of years – and one tree going through all of them. The coal seams are interspersed with layers of sand.

Pardon me, but I have an awkward question. If it took hundreds of thousands of years to deposit each layer of sediment around the tree trunk, then why didn't the trunk first decay away?

OR DO YOU THINK THE SEDIMENT LAYERS WERE BUILT UP RAPIDLY?

Since the bottom of the pine tree is the same age as the top of the tree, these layers cannot represent accumulating time.

(Photo: Creation Research, 2003)

Now, lest someone say that polystrates (vertical fossil trees standing upright through many layers) are a rarity, let me place it on record that they are common... and found in large numbers on all continents.

Also, strata builds sideways!

Experiments on sedimentology were carried out at the State University of Colorado, under the direction of French geologist Guy Berthault. [7]

During the process, the larger particles collected horizontally at the bottom of each layer, then graded upwards according to the size of particles in each layer.

This showed that the idea of superposition does not in fact apply to rock strata as previously thought. The experiments indicate that the sedimentary layers on our earth are likely to have *formed sideways under water* in sloping strata series, and not vertically one on top of the other.

Hence the strata *cannot be used to date rocks and fossils*, since different layers were deposited simultaneously.

Perhaps you have already seen this. But if not, one of these days, why not go down to some beach with a small stream running down through it, a stream which carries and deposits sediment? And look closely at how sediment strata REALLY forms.

You will notice that as water carries sand to deposit it, that one layer of sand does NOT deposit on top of another layer. It does not build up from bottom to top. It builds onto it SIDEWAYS. And at the same time layers form – which grow sideways.

Would it amaze you to learn that after the Mount St. Helens eruption of May 18, 1980, sedimentary rock built up 600 feet (180 metres) deep in just a few months – and it was LAYERED![6]

Jack, it's not the way we've been told in school!

And here are some more surprising facts:

NO TIME LAPSE BETWEEN STRATA
1. **Absence of great erosion**:
    Take the Grand Canyon as an example.

    If the horizontal sedimentary layers were really separated by vast periods of time, lying exposed for millions of years, there should be evidence of enormous erosion in the layers.

    You would expect to find deep irregular cuts and other signs of erosion **within** the different layers. Instead, such features are the exception, rather than the rule.

    While there is significant erosion surface between some rock strata in the Grand Canyon, this is consistent with very rapid erosion in soft, "non-hardened" rock.

    Pardon this dumb question...

    But where is the evidence of canyons and river valleys which must have been cut through the strata many times in millions of years?

    (This is what happens in the real world. For example, the Colorado Plateau has been cut through several thousand feet, virtually from top to bottom, by "young" rivers in what geologists admit is recent geological time.)

2. **No time boundaries between strata**:
    The rocks from different "ages" have a uniform physical appearance. There are no physical differences in structure or appearance.
    That's right. Physically there is no way to distinguish one "age" from another, except by its fossils. You see, all of those successive layers show no physical evidence at all of any time boundaries.
    A single formation of limestone will often contain fossils that are theoretically several geological "ages" apart; with no evidence of any time having elapsed between them.
    Although a formation may be capped by a physical break, if you trace it out laterally far enough you will eventually see it grading imperceptibly into another formation – which therefore succeeds it continuously and rapidly without a time break at that point.
    It is a well recognised fact that there is rarely ever a clear physical boundary between formations.
    More commonly, rock types tend to merge and mingle with each other over a depth of considerable thickness.
    Since there is no dividing line in the rocks between the presumed ages, and each merges imperceptibly into the next, with no evident time lapse from one sediment layer to another, may one reasonably conclude that they were formed in quick succession (perhaps even in one event?)

3. **Deposited in quick succession**:
    Many times the bodies of animals (such as crocodiles, sharks and fish, like those in Whitby Museum, England, are PRESSED DEAD FLAT by the huge weight of the layers of sediments above them.
    This could only have happened if the strata containing them were still soft, while layers were piling up above to crush them.
    This proves that large volumes of sediments were DEPOSITED RAPIDLY in quick succession.
    Supporting this is the fact that all over the world, numerous separate strata are together bent and folded. Bent rock layers are

evidence that those successive rock layers were all still *soft* when they got bent.

4. **Not exposed to meteorites for very long**

Meteors (chunks of rock from outer space) bombard the earth constantly. The minority of these that actually reach the earth we call meteorites.

If the rock layers of our planet took millions of years to be laid down, then they have been open to meteors for millions of years, right? So accumulating meteors would be embedding in the strata during this time, right? And they would be incorporated into these rock layers today, right?

But here I am – and call me a spoil sport, if you like - insisting quite the opposite. I'm saying that the geological strata column was laid down quickly, under catastrophic conditions.

If so, it could not have been exposed to meteorites for very long.

So there should be very few meteorites in the geologic column. Finding a meteorite in the rock strata should be a rare occurrence.

Okay then, here are the two predictions:

a) **The evolutionary theory** predicts a high number of meteorites. They should turn up fairly often in geological research.

b) **My rapid formation theory** predicts a very small number of meteorites in the geologic column. So finding one should be an extremely rare event.

So, what is found… really?

One survey of the literature a few years ago failed to turn up a single case of a meteorite being found in the geologic column.[8]

Prove me wrong, if you can. The meteorite "clock" reads clearly that the geological column is *not very old*.

No evidence for long aeons of time? You got it!.

THE GEOLOGICAL "AGES" NEVER EXISTED

The progressive evolution-of-life fossil column is purely imagination.

You ask, then how could it have got accepted so easily?

Here's how. It became entrenched in the teaching system BEFORE geological research had been extensively done in most of the world.

But it has since been discovered that there is NOT A SINGLE SPOT ON EARTH where the whole series of the different strata (supposedly successive in time) appears. We NEVER find them all together one above another in the same locality.

Nothing resembling such a series has EVER been found together anywhere. Does that shock you?

In no place are more than a handful of the numerous "ages" found. And these few may be any of the numerous theoretical "ages". And they are not always in the expected order.

Even the walls of the Grand Canyon include only five of the twelve major systems (one, five, six and seven, with small portions here and there of the fourth system, the Devonian).

So the evolutionary chart of the succession of life is a **purely artificial theory**. It does not exist anywhere in nature.

George, we've been had!

17

How rock strata formed -
WHAT MY TEACHER DIDN'T KNOW

I sat in class listening as Mr Espiner, my high school science teacher – a genial man he was, too - explained that land animals got buried either by wading into shallow sea or lake water, or by river floods. Then their bones became fossilised.

He explained it all very clearly.

The land slowly slipped under the ocean and was covered with marine sediment. Then it rose **very slowly** again.

Regular series of strata, he told us, were formed by the land slowly rising and sinking again over aeons of time.

And he added, "Sediment building goes on forever in the sea."

Sounds reasonable? Let's go out and prove it in the real world. Surely it has to be true what they're teaching us. So our question as we start digging is:

HOW DID FOSSIL-BEARING STRATA FORM?
1. *Sediment not uniform in depth:*
   Wait a minute, here is a problem. Core samples have shown that some parts of the ocean bottom have almost no sedimentary rock.
   Yet, on land, sediment is up to tens of thousands of feet thick.
   Read that again. Do you see? Something is wrong here!

2. *Raised many times and still horizontal?:*
   Something else. Large areas of sediments containing marine fossils are **almost perfectly horizontal.** Yes, believe it or not, horizontal even three miles above sea level, as, for example, in the Tibetan highlands.
   According to evolutionism, these strata were alternately sunk and uplifted again innumerable times – as well as thousands of feet vertically – over long ages.
   Yet they are perfectly horizontal. How come?

Here's another example: the Colorado Plateau, through which now cuts the Grand Canyon. Here some 250,000 square miles had to go through numerous cycles of uplift and submergence, so we're told. Yet they are still marvellously horizontal.

May I ask, please, how was this large area uplifted from far below sea level to over a mile above sea level, without disturbing the horizontality of the layers? And remember, this had to happen, subsiding, then rising again, not once, but many, many times!

Is this what happened? Of course not.

Do you see? Here are thousands of square miles of horizontal strata, thousands of feet thick.

Might I suggest that a huge Flood rapidly deposited sediment-laden water over this vast area of horizontal layers? Doesn't that make some sense?

And don't let the size of the Grand Canyon bother you. It didn't need millions of years to cut it out. In Book 3 of this series, *The Corpse Came Back*, I shall show you just how rapidly a canyon can form. It will amaze you!

3. *Gradual submergence?:*

The truth is, nothing presently occurring can explain the magnitude of the ocean overflow of the past.

And here's something else that's very important. In fact, it's crucial: Adjacent areas provide **insufficient material** for such enormous deposition.

Clearly, something unusual happened in the past to produce this abundant sediment.

Oh, and another thing. Gradual formation of rock layers ought to have provided a more uniform distribution of fossils. But such is not the case. Most rock formations have no fossils at all. Fossils occur in isolated pockets, in just the manner that a catastrophe would deposit them.

FOSSILS STILL FORMING NOW?

You know, it is quite amazing that fossils exist at all. Today we never see great graveyards of animals mixed together awaiting fossilisation.

Two hundred years ago countless numbers of bison roamed North America. Huge numbers died from prairie fires, quicksand and other natural causes. In an area 100 by 25 miles near the Brazos River, several million starved to death. Yet NO BONES of these modern bison became fossils in sedimentary rocks, and scarcely any are found in a state of preservation. Dredging of sediment from the Mississippi River, the English Channel and other places has revealed virtually nothing in the way of buried skeletons.

When land animals die, all parts tend to disintegrate relatively fast. It is practically impossible to find bones of modern animals in the process of fossilisation. Fossils do still form (generally marine), but only under limited conditions.

In the sea

The constant churning up of the sea floor by marine organisms prevents a tranquil build-up of sediment with which to bury remains.

Neither are ocean currents washing clay, sand and other materials from one place to another to form true stratified beds. **If the ocean floor were uplifted, we would NOT see strata containing fossils.**

Ocean currents do not affect the depths; they affect only a few hundred feet near the surface.

Geologists now realise that conditions in the deep waters are entirely unlike the records in the strata.

On land

Worms and other creatures act upon soil to prevent a tranquil buildup of sediment to bury remains.

And modern rivers are not making layers of rock like those we find from the past. They are dumping mainly fine mud into the sea (unlike the gravel and other material of the past).

The theory of evolution depends on an idea called uniformitarianism. That is, that all things have continued uniformly without interruption over millions of years, to produce all that exists today.

"UNIFORMITY" THEORY IS INADEQUATE

The renowned naturalist Georges Cuvier was the founder of vertebrate paleontology, the science relating to fossil animals. Studying finds from around Europe, he came to the conclusion that "none of the agents which she [Nature] now employs, would have been sufficient for the production of her ancient works."[1]

Thickness of sediment

It has been scientifically estimated that over 75 percent of the earth's surface is sedimentary in nature (the balance being of volcanic origin).

This sediment is miles deep in places. Imagine sediment to fill a whole 8 miles (12 km) deep! This is common, not the exception. The deepest sedimentary deposit thus far found is in India – 60,000 feet deep! In the U.S.A., oil wells have been drilled 25,000 feet down into the sediment.

No present process is capable of explaining the source or origin of these deep deposits of sediment. Dr. L.H. Adams called this one of the major unsolved problems of geology.[2]

Dr. George C. Kennedy, Professor of Geology at U.C.L.A., goes further:

"These deep troughs filled with sediments may contain 50,000 to 100,000 feet of sediments and may be 1000 or more miles long and 100 miles in width."[3]

SUCH SEDIMENT SUGGESTS A MASSIVE GLOBAL FLOOD

Such sediments are to be expected if the waters of a universal Flood ever covered the earth.

A global maelstrom of storm-whipped tidal waves could transport material for hundreds of miles and fill depressions, whatever the height or extent of nearby landscapes.

The rock strata reveals that the earth's surface must have been torn up for miles down and relaid by the action of water. The earth's crust was churned into a mass of water, vegetation, animal life and soil sediment.

So violent was the Flood that not only were surface soil and minerals mixed with vegetation and animal life; the deeper strata of the original crust was also broken up. Thus layers of primeval gypsum, dolomite and anhydrate suffered breakup and were redeposited alternately with fossil-bearing surface materials.

And in this manner we find them.

The character, texture and colour of the rocks of individual strata would differ according to the locality from which the material was moved. Sometimes it would measure but a few feet in thickness, and elsewhere up to thousands of feet, depending on the depth of the basin to which it was carried. From place to place, material varied from clay, gravel and sand, to boulders, volcanic ash, ooze from an uplifted ocean bed, or loess. At times it was carefully assorted into strata.

In the numerous layers, revealed in the rock strata, we find sandstone, coal, shale, limestone – and these layers in some places have been repeated up to 70 times.

Elsewhere it was buried together in wild confusion, as in smaller floods today.

During all this period, the laws of nature governing water, tides and waves were active.

This strata on the North Fork of the Toutle River south west of Spirit Lake formed in one day. (Creation Ex Nihilo magazine, Vol.15, No.3)

Repeating cycles were formed by mighty currents sweeping in masses of debris, in a brief span of time. Travelling long distances under water, fast-moving currents of suspended mud spread out over thousands of square miles.

Can strata form rapidly? Yes. The photo on the previous page, taken shortly after the Mount St Helens eruption above shows 25 feet (8 metres) of thick layers that were formed in one day – and more probably in just three hours! It was formed by flowing 'rivers' of volcanic ash (not lava) moving at speeds of 100 miles (160 kilometres) an hour.

FOSSILS LIKEWISE SUGGEST A GREAT FLOOD

The supposed proofs of evolution can be more satisfactorily interpreted in terms of Creation and the Flood. The evolution theory's unresolved difficulties are indeed positive evidence for some other explanation.

The fossil record is not at all a record of gradual evolution over long ages at all, but rather the chronicle, written in the rocks, of the sudden destruction of life – of the terrible events of a single year, the year of the Great Flood.

The geological time scale will eventually be seen as the most incredible misinterpretation of scientific data in the history of geology, if not in the history of science.

The obviously **catastrophic** source of the earth's strata, the manner in which it was laid down, renders the evolutionary geological time-scale **meaningless**.

The fossils testify to SUDDEN death and RAPID burial before they could be dismembered by normal decay processes.

The event is soberly recorded in Genesis:

"Every living creature that moves on earth perished, birds, cattle, wild animals, all reptiles, and all mankind. Everything died that had the breath of life in its nostrils, everything on dry land. God wiped out every living thing that existed on earth, man and beast, reptile and bird; they were all wiped out over the whole earth, and only Noah and his company in the ark survived."[4]

For 150 days, mighty earth-shaping forces continued to destroy and remould. Volcanic activity was intense, sometimes interspersing lava flows between sediments laid down by tidal return. Mountains were made and unmade, and countless varieties of phenomena were formed, which puzzle students of geology today. Without the facts of the Genesis Flood, historical geology is a waste of time.

As the sediment settled, it hardened into stone. In this stone are the petrified forms of animals and vegetation... the fossils.

THE FLOOD ACTED DIFFERENTLY IN DIFFERENT LOCALITIES

While the destruction of the face of the earth was total and complete, the forces were not equal in all areas. The result was variation in the effects of the Deluge from place to place.

In some localities the Flood sediment might be only a few feet in thickness. But where pre-Flood basins were filled up it could reach thousands of feet deep.

BASEMENT ROCK MIXED WITH FLOOD SEDIMENT

The bulk of the fossil-bearing sedimentary rocks probably formed during the opening and closing stages of the Flood, with lesser amounts being formed during the long period of subsidence adjustment and run-off after the Flood. The long term geological effects of the Flood apparently lasted for centuries, with extensive volcanism during the Flood, continuing during the post-Flood period.

During and after the Flood, volcanic magma was able to intrude into sedimentary formations. It could also have brought up basement rock to mix and interact with Flood-related volcanic and sedimentary material. If the magma temperature was not too high, then the composite rock would contain unmelted fragments of many rocks through which the magma had passed.

Moreover, during and after the Flood, there were many instances where heat and pressure (from hot gases and molten rock deep in the earth) uplifted granite rock to intrude into recently deposited volcanic and sedimentary material. Hot gases accompanying these solid granite intrusions turned the adjacent sediments into metamorphic rock.

To explain the evidence of worldwide devastation and earth changes, one Flood is adequate. We do not need to speculate more than one. What we see here is evidence of *one Global Flood, with many major upheavals* in the centuries since.

In Book 3 of this series, *The Corpse Came Back*, you will see adequate evidence of the many post-Flood catastrophes and earth movements.

It might be noted that I am comfortable with the possibility that Siberia's frozen mammoths described in Chapter 7 may have been overwhelmed in a post-Flood disaster triggered in the same manner as there described - by a close-passing celestial object.

* * * * * * *

Most of the useful results of geological research remain valid if a Global Flood is accepted. Only the time element and the evolutionary implications are sacrificed. And neither of these has any genuine value in geological research.

There still remain some unsolved problems in connection with so-called "flood geology". However, these are not nearly as difficult to interpret as those confronting the evolutionary geologist. Nor do they require so many auxiliary hypotheses.

So the bottom line is this: THERE IS NO BASIC CONFLICT BETWEEN OBSERVABLE SCIENCE AND GENESIS.

Never before or since the Great Flood has there been such an opportunity for the production of fossils, or for the formation of vast beds of sediment and their conversion into stratified rocks.

From the evidence, then, it is most reasonable and natural to conclude that:
1. Most of the stratified beds containing fossils were formed by the same event.
2. All types of fossil plants and animals were contemporary in the same world, until destroyed by an enormous water catastrophe.
3. The fossils, therefore, demonstrate not a gradual evolution of life over long ages, but rather the sudden extinction, worldwide, of life in one age.

Do the known scientific facts match up with the Bible scenario? In the words of leading physicist Gerald Schroeder, *"Close enough to send chills up your spine"*.[5]

Chills up your spine?

The same goes for the dinosaur evidence. It's not as they've been telling us...

HOW STRATA FORMED - Summary

The **best** proof of evolution, according to most evolutionists, is **the fossils**. The strata of the earth's crust, now solidified into rock, lie upon one another much like layers of a cake. The deeper layers of sediment were laid down first. These usually contain simpler fossils than the shallower rocks. This is proof, we are told, that the first forms of life were small, simple creatures. After long ages of time, these became still higher, until finally appeared present animals, plants and man.

MIXED UP SEQUENCE

However, fossil-bearing strata do **not** everywhere exhibit the same order. In different locations, one can find practically **any sequence** whatever of fossils.
1. Around the world, **every single one** of the different sets of rock is found in the bottom position.
2. Supposedly "older" and simpler fossils are found above layers of "younger," more complex animals.

Even so-called "overthrusts" cannot adequately explain this.

NO TIME LAPSE BETWEEN STRATA

There is no evidence of erosion between strata laid down supposedly millions of years apart. And there is no dividing line in the rocks between the presumed "ages." Furthermore, there is evidence that strata which contained dead creatures had not yet hardened before new layers forming above crushed them. This speaks of rapid deposition of large volumes of sediment in quick succession.

INDIVIDUAL FOSSILS THROUGH SEVERAL STRATA

Trees and animal remains are sometimes found penetrating through many successive rock layers – which had to be laid down rapidly before the organism could decay.

GEOLOGICAL "AGES" ARE IMAGINARY

The theory of a geological progression of fossils was accepted **before** geological research had been extensively made in most of the world. We now know that the pattern simply **cannot** be insisted upon. At **no** place in the world is the complete or even partially complete series of the different strata (said to be successive in time) even known to exist. So the evolutionary chart of the succession of life is a pure fiction! It is simply NOT supported by the geological evidence.

"EARLIEST" FORMS STILL ALIVE

Some animals believed to have been extinct for aeons and **which have been used to date the strata in which they were found**, have since been found very much alive.

MODERN DESCENDANTS UNCHANGED

Modern descendants of the "most ancient" organisms are essentially unchanged – showing no evolution. With few exceptions, the fossils furnish us with a **cross section** of the organisms living at the time the Flood struck. They demonstrate **not** a gradual evolution of life over ages and ages, but rather the sudden extinction, worldwide, of life in one age.

18

Dinosaurs and humans -

DINOSAUR ALIVE!

In the forest areas near Sadiya, in northern Assam, two tea planters were hunting – quite ready, they thought, for anything. They were in for a substantial shock.

The sun was setting. A warm orange glow was spreading its magic over the reeds.

Suddenly, both men were startled. The noises were loud. They were hearing the sounds of a ponderous animal wallowing in the swamp. As they crept toward it, they were amazed to see a reptilian head raise itself on an endless neck above the reeds. The men fired, both of them. Apparently that was useless. The animal simply turned and heaved its vast bulk away to the centre of the swamp, where it could not be followed.

Was this one of the Buru, of which the tribespeople often spoke?

NOT SO VICIOUS

Long ago, extraordinary creatures roamed about freely on our planet.

Today we call them dinosaurs.

Remains were found in South America of a dinosaur that had been as long as 150 feet (46 metres). This "earth shaker" may have weighed as much as 100 tons. By comparison, a modern large bull elephant weighs about 7 tons.

A brontosaurus could drink with ease from the gutter of a two-storied house. And the flying pterandon, 20 feet long, when in the air would look as big as an elephant in flight.

A single dinosaur would probably have eaten up to 400 tons of food a day.

Of course there were also small varieties of dinosaur that were no larger than chickens.

Much new information concerning dinosaurs is coming to light. So much is new that a lot of what you have read or heard about dinosaurs in the past is probably incorrect.

There is no scientific evidence that any dinosaur was as vicious as we have been led to believe. The bones, teeth and stomach contents of fossil dinosaurs tell us that most of them were harmless plant-eaters. We have little evidence to indicate that any of the dinosaurs definitely ate meat. Much more research is needed.

The Tyrannosaurus rex is often pictured as a savage killer. However, its sharp teeth and claws may well have been used to tear up tough plants and fruits. Many sharp-toothed animals living today are plant-eaters which rarely, if ever, eat flesh.

NOT DUMB AND CLUMSY

In 1976, paleontologist Adrian Desmond offered new evidence to suggest that dinosaurs were not slow, clumsy creatures, but swift and graceful and far from stupid. They were highly intelligent, warm-blooded creatures who were marvels of agility and grace.[1]

They were far superior to our surviving reptiles, the komodo dragon and crocodile. It is claimed that the Tyrannosaurus could run as fast as a galloping horse or a charging tiger!

This much is certain: dinosaurs could not have just evolved by mindless chance. As more and more fossils of these astonishing creatures are discovered – some as long as 40 metres (130 feet) – one is amazed at their wonderful design. The Brachiosaurus, as tall as a four story building, had a neck which was built just like the jib of a crane! Its design shows an intelligent plan.

DINOSAURS NOT MILLIONS OF YEARS AGO

One thing that is basic to the evolution theory is this: that the dinosaur evolved and then became extinct millions of years before there were any people on earth. It is very strongly held that no man ever saw a dinosaur.

Age of dinosaur fossils

But what do the fossil remains of dinosaurs show us? Does it really take millions, or even thousands, of years for something to become fossilised?

Well, how about this? Did you know that chicken bones and wood have been found to fossilise in just 5 to 10 years? A large dinosaur bone might take hundreds of years to completely fossilise. All that is required is the right minerals, quick burial and the right amount of water.

In fact, many dinosaur bones are composed of less than 50 percent rock; the rest is original bone. This is clear evidence of burial within the last few thousand years.[2]

Did you know that FRESH, unfossilised dinosaur bones have been found? In 1987, a young Inuit (Canadian Eskimo) working on Bylot Island with scientists from Memorial University, Newfoundland, found a bone which was identified as part of a lower jaw of a duckbill dinosaur.

And in 1981, fresh bones found in Alaska were identified as belonging to horned dinosaurs, duckbill dinosaurs, and small carnivorous dinosaurs.[3]

More surprises! In some dinosaur bones, proteins and amino acids can still be found. Dinosaur bones have yielded the protein osteocalcin. Since long chains such as proteins also naturally fall apart, such a discovery supports a "recent" age for dinosaurs.[4]

ALL THEORIES INADEQUATE

At least 55 different theories have been put forth as to why the dinosaurs disappeared. One by one, these theories have fallen.

As Edwin H. Colbert says:

"The great extinction that wiped out all of the dinosaurs, large and small, in all parts of the world, and at the same time... was an event that has defied all attempts at a satisfactory explanation."[5]

One commentator summed it up perfectly:
"All theories on the dinosaurs' extinction are now extinct."[6]
U.C. Berkeley physicist, Luis Alverez says:
"The problem is not what killed the dinosaurs but what killed almost all the life at the time."[7]

The great dinosaur graveyards found in various parts of the world demand some form of catastrophic action. To those who do not believe in the Great Flood, it is a continuing mystery why the dinosaurs suddenly died.

TAKEN ABOARD THE SURVIVAL VESSEL

Since Noah took on board the Ark at least one set of every air-breathing land animal,[8] dinosaurs must have been included. The Ark certainly had enough space.[9] But it would have been unnecessary to take old, full-sized 80 ton dinosaurs. All he needed was a pair of small youngsters of each basic type.

AFTER THE FLOOD

Dinosaurs certainly survived for some centuries after the Flood. However, in an impoverished new world, there were no longer the great forests and nutritional plant life to sustain them, as before.

Many other large animals also became extinct in the harshness of the new environment.

MAN AND DINOSAUR

The traditions of ancient peoples all over the earth tell us of huge, reptilian creatures strikingly like the dinosaurs. The term "dinosaur" was not invented until 1841. The ancients called them "dragons" or "monsters".

A few hundred years after the Flood it was written in the book of Job that the greatest creature on earth was a monster with a strong tail like the thick, tall trunk of the cedar tree. The name given it was "behemoth".[10] Such a tail disqualifies the elephant or the hippopotamus, but does fit the dinosaur.

Legends

The more ancient stories are more matter-of-fact in quality, while the more recent ones tend to be more fanciful – which would be expected if the dinosaur was now becoming a rarity.

* An old science book, *Historia Animalium*, says that "dragons" lived in Europe as late as the sixteenth century. But the animals were said to be extremely rare and relatively small by then.

* In 900 A.D., an Irish writer reported meeting a huge animal with thick legs, strong claws and "iron" spikes on its back. Was this a Stegosaurus?

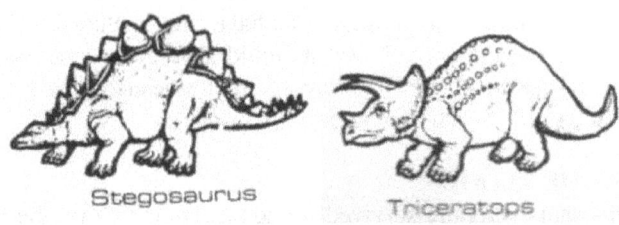

Stegosaurus   Triceratops

* The French city of Nerius changed its name after a "dragon" with long, sharp horns on its head was killed there. It was probably a Triceratops.

* Some old Chinese history books even tell of a family that kept "dragons" and raised their babies. It is said that in those days Chinese kings used "dragons" to pull royal chariots on special occasions.

* Such creatures were battled by Gilgamesh of Babylon (this one was eating forest growth); King Morvidus of Wales about 336 B.C. (who was killed by it); King Peredur of Wales (who slew it at a place called Llyn Llion); Beowulf of Scandinavia about 495-583 A.D. (who killed two, but lost his life at 88 in the process of killing another); Siegfried of the ancient Teutons; Tristan, King Arthur and Sir Lancelot of Britain, and, of course, the famous St. George (c. 300 A.D.). Early records of the fight between St. George and the dragon are much more sober and believable than the popular accounts written later in children's books on fables. There may be some basis of truth in the story.

* Fraser of Glenvackie is credited with having killed the last known "dragon" in Scotland. The date, according to historical records, is about 1520.

* On May 13, 1572, a farmer in northern Italy killed a dinosaur-like creature. It was examined and described by Italian scientist Ulysses Aldrovandas.

My files are jam-packed with such reports through history.

There is something striking about these "dragon" or "monster" reports and legends:
1. They exist virtually worldwide.
2. There are many items of similarity between the creatures slain and known dinosaur fossils.

Many ancient armies used the dragon ensign. It was often the chief among royal ensigns in war.

Drawings

Archaeologists occasionally find ancient drawings of animals that look very much like dinosaurs. In fact, hundreds of dinosaur pictures have been found around the world. For example:

* In Zimbabwe, the Amazon valley and Arizona, dinosaur pictographs have been found on cave or canyon walls, rock outcrops and boulders. In Bolivia they appear on ancient ceramic pottery. In Ecuador they have been found on stone plaques.

* In Ica, Peru, genuine ancient stone engravings clearly show man and dinosaur as cosy neighbours. Human beings are portrayed hunting or struggling with monsters resembling triceratops, stegosaurs and pterodactyls. Others show people as having domesticated animals that appear to be dinosaurs; they are using them for warfare and transportation.

* Ancient Indians in Peru prepared stones to be placed in tombs. The burial stones were of scenes from everyday life and included many pictures of dinosaurs, many of them pictures with people and dinosaurs together.

Dr Javiera Cabrera's museum at Ica contains about 11,000 of these rounded stones weighing from 5 pounds (2½ kilograms) to boulders of 800 pounds (c.400 kilograms). Samples of these stones were sent to Spain by the Spanish explorers in 1562. That they are not of recent origin is evidenced by the oxidation produced by ageing which covers the incisions of the drawings.

* Ancient Cocle pottery designs in Panama represent a flying lizard that looks like the extinct pterodactyl. Prehistoric animals are painted along with recognisable animals, according to American archaeologist A. Hyatt Verrill.[11]
* In Mexico, in July, 1945, near Acambaro in the state of Guanajuato, a chance discovery of clay figurines was made by amateur archaeologist Waldemar Julsind. These were found at the base of Blue Mountain in shallow burials dated to at least 1,500 years old. In all, 30,000 fragments were unearthed. These included ancient ceramic models of people and animals which resemble dinosaur-like reptiles.

Many of them depict animals that strongly resemble camels, elephants, horses-- animals no longer found in the area-- but also exact replications of Stegosaurus, Tyrannosaurus Rex and Pterodactyls thought to have been extinct for over 60 million years!

Some of the giant saurians are shown with women in non-hunting, non-violent situations, perhaps as pets or domestic animals. The humans wear laced sandals, shields and chain mail.

In this instance, some disrepute was attached to the discovery, because it was found that after the publicity local inhabitants set about salting prospective digs with home-made clay dinosaurs of their own.

Though few archaeologists or anthropologists have bothered to examine the ancient specimens, they are automatically dismissed as outrageous fakes.

There should have been no artisan of ancient Mexico with the faintest idea that dinosaurs had even existed, let along what they looked like. A number of these are now in display at the local museum.

* In 1924, on a wall of the Havasupai Canyon in the Grand Canyon area of Arizona, the Doheny expedition discovered a carving of a Tyrannosaurus rex, standing upright.

It portrays the creature as supported by his massive tail, ready to use his powerful jaws and fangs on a prospective victim.

This petroglyph high up on the canyon wall is so old that the iron slowly seeping from the rock has formed a protective coating.

In the same canyon another carving, likewise coated in iron patina, shows a man either attacking or defending himself against a mammoth.

* On the next page is a petroglyph of a dinosaur found at Natural Bridges National monument in Utah. It is attributed to the Anasazi Indians who lived in the area from AD 400 to 1300.[12]

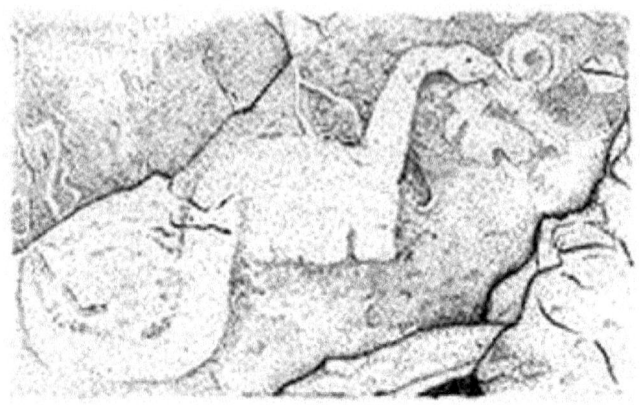

* At Big Sandy River, Oregon, a rock carving can be identified as a stegosaurus. The drawing was made by scratching red sandstone with a flint. It shows evidence of great age.

How absurd it would be to think that an ancient artist would be able to reproduce monsters whose appearance is known to us only from the long researches and meticulous studies of modern experts!

How could "primitive" man have drawn beasts which he had never seen?

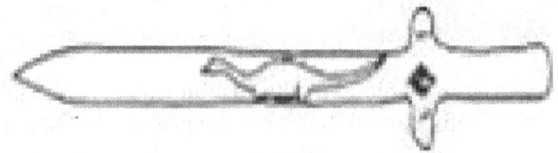

The engraving on this 2,000 year old Roman sword clearly depicts a dinosaur.

Remains found together

In Chapter 13, we touched on a rather startling discovery in the Paluxy River basin, near Glen Rose, Texas, hinting strongly that man and dinosaur had lived together in the area.

One trail of human footprints actually crossed the tracks of the dinosaurs.

Carbon-dating of this stratum gave readings of only a few thousand years. Although I do not place too much faith in carbon dating (for reasons given in *The Killing of Paradise Planet*), I mention these readings because carbon dating is regularly appealed to as evidence by those who hold the established view.

Adjacent to the tracks, on the same Cretaceous layer, there was a long black streak of a fallen tree branch which had been burned to charcoal prior to burial in the limey surface. About 7 feet long and 2 inches in diameter, it was embedded some 200 metres downstream from the human and dinosaur tracks. A section of this branch was extracted for carbon-14 analysis. R. Berger, a geophysicist at U.C.L.A., later pronounced the branch to be 12,800 years old.

Thus, in this stratum we have evidence of dinosaurs contemporaneous with early man and dateable by a tree branch as being no more than 13,000 years ago! By its own criteria, it seems that the whole science of geochronology as conventionally practised is due for a complete overhaul.

Now naturally these exhibits will not be popular with some people. The majority of the scientific community has greeted them with deathly silence because of early indoctrination in evolution. It tries to ignore them for the sole reason that it cannot explain them.

DINOSAURS LIVING TODAY?

It is difficult to say categorically that any animal is extinct. Several times geologists have been severely embarrassed, when, after having declared animals to be extinct, they have been discovered alive and well.

On the remote island of Komodo in Indonesia are about a thousand "prehistoric" monster lizards, the Komodo "dragons". They were totally unknown to modern man until the year 1912! Scientists have been perplexed by this mystery: One of the "oldest" animals on earth is found on a geologically "young" island. How did it get there?

There is some evidence that a few dinosaurs and great marine reptiles could still be alive today, still teetering on the edge of extinction.

Plesiosaurs (deep water dinosaurs)

In 1977, Japanese fishing nets off New Zealand caught the decaying body of a large, strange reptile. Photographs, measurements and tissue samples suggested it was probably one of the great marine reptiles like the Plesiosaurus.

The Japanese government issued a stamp to commemorate this catch.

All over the world, ship captains have reported animals like this, as well as other types of unknown sea monsters. There have been hundreds of such accounts.

The *Melbourne Sun* of February 6, 1980 noted that more than forty people had claimed to have seen plesiosaurs off the Victorian coast over the previous twelve years.

All around the world, many reliable observers have sketched or described sea creatures which resemble ancient plesiosaurs or ichthyosaurs, dragon-like monsters apparently still alive in the abyssal depths. Such reports, I should point out, often come from people whose integrity or soundness of mind would not otherwise be questioned.

In 1952, Fred Olsen was patrolling the Esperanza Inlet area for the Canadian Department of Fisheries. He recounts:

"The Canadian Fishing Company had a fish buying camp at Queens Cove, near the entrance to Esperanza inlet. The 'camp' was a 90 ft. scow with two decks, the lower contained the fish storage space and ice house, the upper the living quarters. Part of the upper deck was open, similar to a sun-deck.

"The scow was moored to pilings away from shore, and lived in by the manager, his wife and three children. One day, while working on the sun-deck, which was some 10 feet above the sea, the man spotted a moving object out of the corner of his eye... his first impression was that one of the black creosoted pilings had somehow worked loose and was falling over, alongside the camp, into the sea. Startled, he wheeled around, and the sight that met his eyes shocked him more than anything he had ever experienced in his adventurous life. On an eel-like neck, thicker than a piling, a head with enormous eyes, towering six feet above the sun-deck, was passing very slowly by the camp. Electrified into action, he tore through the doorway into the living quarters, and seized his 30-30 rifle, which he kept loaded at all times. By now the dreadful thing had reached the outside window of the living quarters, and his wife and daughter were gaping in horror....

"As the camp man dashed back to the sun-deck, he slammed the door behind him. Apparently startled, the creature turned its head towards the window and opened its mouth widely and mother and daughter were treated to the spectacle of a huge pink-lined mouth and frightful, shark-like teeth. The thing slid slowly out of view and the two rushed to the window... below, slightly underwater, was passing the enormous whale-sized body of the monster. Whale-like too, were the huge 12 foot wide flukes, slowly propelling the appalling creature through the water....

"Out on deck, the man... sighted on the back of the animal's head, a mere 20 feet away... he hesitated; somewhere he had heard of the peanut sized brain of dinosaurs. This thing resembled a dinosaur... he knew that if he failed to paralyse or kill the thing with one shot, the titanic convulsions of the monster would probably smash the camp to pieces and bring destruction upon them all.

"He did not shoot. The animal submerged slowly, its great body visible underwater as it moved towards the head of the cove... A chill February breeze was blowing from the Pacific, but it was not the cold which made him shiver violently. His body was drenched with perspiration! The head of the cove was covered with ice about an inch thick. There was a slight splintering sound as the thing appeared again. It reared up about a dozen feet through and above the ice and turned its head in all directions... Then it sank again, to be seen no more.

"Recovering from the shock of the experience the witnesses rowed over to another camp-boat, but their story was met with incredulity. The camp men made a sketch of what they had seen and sent it to the Department of Fisheries biological station at Nanaimo – who replied that no such creature existed, and that he had probably seen a sea-cow... The weird story was ridiculed everywhere and in the end the family subsided into angry silence."[13]

Many well documented accounts are in my files. Often the reptiles are described as having heads like those of alligators. Marine reptiles with heads like alligators are said to have existed along with the dinosaurs "millions" of years ago.

In lakes and rivers
Over the years there have been consistent reported sightings of plesiosaur-like monsters in lakes in:
- Sweden (Lake Storsjon)
- Scotland (several lakes, including Loch Ness, which has an underwater outlet to the sea.)
- Ireland (Loughs Fee, Bran, Much, Bray, Dub, Neagh, Cleevaun, Nacorra and Glendalaugh)
- Canada (Lakes Okanagan, Simcoe and Winnipegosis)
- U.S.A. (Lake Payett, Idaho)
- Eastern Siberia (Lakes Vorota, Khaiyr and Labynkyr)

On land
* In the 1800s, missionaries in Africa reported a trail of large three-clawed footprints unlike those of any known African animal.
* North Assam: The Apa Thani tribe in a remote upland valley of northern Assam had a strong tradition of a "buru" (monster) which existed in a large swamp nearby. It used to put its long neck up out of the water and make a hoarse, bellowing noise. Their ancestors drained the swamp and killed the burus. They still point out three burial sites where the last three burus were buried.

Some 200 miles southwest, another tribe describe the same animal as still in existence and frequently seen in a swamp valley called Rilo. This virtually unexplored mountain territory is claimed by both India and China.
* Malaysia: There are several reports from the Semelai people concerning a large lake in the remote centre of the Malay Peninsula. A part of the lake known as Tasek Bera is surrounded by tall reeds. Large animals are said to inhabit the lake. Their necks are described as tall as a palm tree and fully 6 feet thick. Sometimes the tail is seen, but the body always remains under water.

An officer of the Malay police reported an unnerving experience. One afternoon, when bathing, he looked back toward shore and noticed a massive "snake's" head rising above a 15 foot clump of Russau palm. Its slate-coloured body was enormously thick. In panic, he raced for his boat, and as he rowed away, could see the monster watching him, unconcerned.[14]

* South America: Natives of the Madre de Dios region in eastern Peru, a wild, unexplored region in the upper Amazon headwaters, describe a dinosaur-like creature which they claim inhabits swampy jungle land several days' walk in from the river.

The famed British explorer Colonel P.H. Fawcett, was employed as surveyor for South American governments in the border regions of Brazil, Bolivia and Peru. He reached the eastern edge of Madre de Dios, a country of swamps. One day, while running his dug-outs through it, he saw a great reptilian head rise out of the jungle, but before he could shoot, the head was lowered. From the noise the creature made getting away, he took it to be some sort of dinosaur. His native carriers revolted and he had to get out of the area quickly.

Fawcett believed the animal might be Diplodocus, the 80-foot reptile of 25 tons. It was an eater of aquatic plants, which grow profusely in this region.

The Diplodocus story is confirmed by many of the tribes east of the River Ucayali.

Former American intelligence offer Leonard Clark penetrated the same dangerous region of the western Amazon in the 1940s.

He asked the Indians if they had seen any large animals lately. He was informed that years before it was common to see very large animals on the east bank come out of the jungle to drink. Idly, he asked about their size. He recalls:

"This brave pointed to a tree about forty feet high! All these riverine tribes have legends of such beasts existing in the jungle lying out towards the Brazilian frontier. Except for a few clans living on the rivers, these jungle tracts are completely uninhabited; at least so say the Chamas. Can any man say what lies out there?"[15]

* Africa: Explorers and natives in a very remote jungle in the Congo repeatedly tell of sightings of a large dinosaur-like animal.[16] Various sightings have been reported from Lake Tele, a

shallow oval lake about 4 by 5 kilometres, with swamp forest all around the edge.

Occasional visitors over the last 200 years have all confirmed that the natives are absolutely honest in their reports of the "mokele-mbembe" which are huge, with small heads, long necks, and long, massive tails. They have been described as "half elephant and half dragon".

In 1959, some of the pigmies say, they speared one to death. All who ate it, died soon afterward. When shown pictures of various large animals, living and extinct, the natives have always verified the brontosaurus as closest in appearance to "mokele-mbembe"!

In the early 1980s, there were several expeditions into this forbidding Likouala swamp region, located in the northern part of the Congo.

Scientist Roy Mackal of the University of Chicago, investigated the reports coming out of the area personally. He showed various pictures to the natives in the area. Only when he showed them pictures of the sauropods and of the Brontosaurus did they identify its shape.[17]

Natives claimed it was living along the rivers and deep swamp pools. A vegetarian, the creature will fight with hippos over a territory rich in molombo plants. They described the creature as brownish-grey, with short, thick legs, and weighing probably about 9 to 15 tons. It was about 35 feet from its small head to its tail. Although it had killed fishermen, it had not eaten them.[18]

According to a later report by Dick Donovan of Associated Press, space scientist Herman Regusters claimed that his expedition into those remote African jungles sighted a gigantic dinosaur. The creature raised its head out of the water and travelled for a quarter of a mile, before diving beneath the surface. They sighted it again four hours later. His expedition returned with droppings, footprint casts and sound recording unlike any animal known to the Congo Basin area.

Another expedition to the African Congo, this time led by Marcellin Agnagna, a biologist, reported another sighting of a dinosaur-like animal.[19]

The *Sunday Times of London* reported in May of 1999 that members of the Kabonga tribe actually killed a mokele-mbembe!

Late in 2000 an expedition led by Genesis Park staff slogged through "nasty swamps, floating jungle rivers, trekking virgin rain forests and interviewing pygmy forest peoples who had never before talked to an outside explorer. From village to village informants recognized this creature from a lineup of various animals. The name was always the same: 'Li'kela-bembe.' Eyewitnesses led them to places where it had been seen, in some cases quite recently. Its actions were described in fascinating detail and in harmony with Dr. Mackal's information from the Congo."[20]

Extensive research has established the authenticity of many reports. For other reports there is almost total lack of supporting evidence. However, there is a hard core of evidence which one cannot honestly dismiss as misidentification, error or hoax.

The modern "plesiosaur" and "ichthyosaur" sightings are either in waterways connected to the sea or in lakes around the world that were once connected to the ocean. Retreating waters from the Great Flood left pockets of remote, but adequate, water tracts in which such animals were stranded.

In a few remote, undisturbed areas where vegetative luxuriance persists, it seems quite possible that dinosaurs still survive.

EPILOGUE

I THOUGHT OF THAT BUILDING BURIED TWO MILES DEEP IN A COAL SEAM. And the baleen whale in the Lompoc quarry... the SURPRISE WITNESS to an event irresistibly violent; so violent that this 80 foot monster was tipped up on its tail inside hundreds of feet of swirling sediments and buried so quickly it could'nt even fall over.

Yes, we're talking about a Deluge of unparalleled proportions. Not only did it sweep away the original super civilization... this Flood event leaves the evolution theory all wet!

In the popular interpretation of history there is no place for a worldwide Flood, because the dating clocks would have to be reset. If the earth's strata were deposited in the rapid, catastrophic manner I have just described, the fossil record becomes totally meaningless, as far as proving evolution is concerned.

A worldwide Flood straddles evolutionary history like a colossus.

But the implications are more staggering still. If the evidence vindicates the scorned biblical documents on this crucial, most assailed point, could it do so on other points?

Might it be time to reassess the role of those biblical writings, as a credible source of history?

If so, are we prepared to consider their claim that the Great Flood was a planned, direct intervention of the Creator in world history – a judgment upon a world which was getting ready to eliminate the last remaining defenders of right living?

And that this handful of survivors was picked to repopulate the planet and give it a new start?

The same Scriptures insist that the Creator does have claims on the population of this planet – not as a stern dictator waiting to dump calamities on peoples' heads, but as a caring, beneficent Father, who desires only our happiness and safety.

And these documents predict that he has scheduled a final interruption to world history – to take over rulership and restore this planet to its original happy state.

Well, might that be better than our present self-imposed mess ... what do you think?

NOTES

Chapter 1 – THE DAY IT ENDED

1. Agassiz, "*Etudes sur les glaciers*," p.311; Cuvier, "*Recherches sur les assements fossils*", 2nd ed., I, 202. Cited by Velikovsky, *Earth in Upheaval*, p.106
2. *Geological Magazine*, 1878, p.265
3. Harold Jeffreys, *The Earth*, p. 303
4. Velikovsky, p.118
5. http://www.holoscience.com
6. *Hist.Sin.* lib.I., p.12
7. The *Harris Papyrus*; the *Hermitage Papyrus*; the *Ipuwer Papyrus*

Chapter 2 – EXPLOSION FROM HELL

1. See the special note at the end of this chapter.
2. *The Book of Jasher*. New York; M.M. Noah and A.S. Gould, 1840. Transl. c.1830, ch.6 v.11
3. Edward Suess, *Face of the Earth*, I, 17ff. Cited by Price, *The New Geology*, p.244
4. Alfred M. Rehwinkel, *The Flood*. St. Louis, Mo.: Concordia Publishing House, 1951, p.103
5. Ibid, p.105
6. Gen. 7:11
7. Genesis 7:11
8. There are 20,000 Pacific Ocean floor volcanoes alone
9. Gen 8:2

10 Frank Lewis Marsh, *Life, Man and Time*, p.95
11 "Mechanism of Formation of Pillow Lava," *American Scientist*, vol.63, May-June, 1975, p.269
12 W.J. Miller, *An Introduction to Historical Geology*, 5th ed., 2nd printing, 1946, p.355
13 Velikovsky, p.83
14 Gregory, "The African Rift Valleys," *Geographical Journal*, LVI, 1920, 31ff
15 This applies to magmas having crystallised at pressures indicative of 1,220 to 3,650 metres depths and temperatures not in excess of 870°C., K. Krauskopi, *Introduction to Geochemistry*. New York: McGraw Hill Book Company, 1967, pp.430-432
16 Carl E. Baugh, *Panorama of Creation*, Fort Worth, *Texas:Creation*, Publication Services, 1992, pp.82-84

Chapter 3 – WAVES AS FAST AS JET PLANES

1 R.F. Flint, *Glacial Geology and the Pleistocene Epoch* 1947, pp.116-117
2 R.F. Flint, *Glacial Geology and the Pleistocene Epoch* (1947), pp. 116-117
3 G.F. Wright, *The Ice Age in North America and Its Bearing upon the Antiquity of Man*, 5th ed; 1911, pp. 238-239
4 G.F. Wright, *The Ice Age in North America and its Bearing Upon the Antiquity of Man*, 5th ed; 1911, pp. 238-239
5 Velikovsky, p.127
6 Horace Benedict de Saussure, *Voyages dans les Alpes*, I, 1779, 151
7 See E.H. Shackleton, *The Heart of the Antarctic*, II, 1909, illustration opposite p. 293
8 Thomas King, *Water*, p.49. New York: Macmillan Co., 1953

9   Willard Bascom, "Ocean Waves," *Scientific American*, vol.201, August 1959, pp.81-83
10 Chile Earthquake Spreads Disaster Around the World," *Civil Engineering*, vol.30, July 1960, p.88
11 *Guinnes Book of Records*, 1986, p.59
12 John Strong, *The Doomsday Globe*, p.104
13 Robert L. Dietz, "Astroblemes," *Scientific American*, August 1961
14 Velikovsky, *Earth in Upheaval*, p.85
15 Upham, *The Glacial Lake Agassiz*, 1895, p.239

Chapter 4 – STAMPEDE

1   Velikovsky, *Earth in Upheaval*, p.195
2   Gen. 7:17-20, literal translation
3   Gen.8:5

Chapter 5 – UNNATURAL GRAVEYARDS

1   Prestwich, "On Certain Phenomena," Idem, *Philosophical Transactions of the Royal Society*, 1893, pp.37-38
2   Velikovsky, p.54
3   Prestwich, p.38
4   H. de Lumley, S. Gagniere, L. Barral, R. Pascal. 1913 "La Grotte du Vallonet, Roquebrune-Cap-Martin, A-M, Note preliminaire", *Bulletin du Musee Anthropologic Prehistorique de Monaco*, vol.10, pp.5-20
5   A.C. Ramsay 1863 "Bone-cave at Cefn, Fllatshire", *"The Geologist,"* vol.6, p.114
6   H.G. Woodward 1887. *The Geology of England and Wales*, London, 2nd ed., XV 670 pp: see p.543

7   A. Harkness 1870. "On the occurrence of elephant remains in Ireland; *Geological Magazine*, vol. vii, pp. 253-258; p.255

8   Velikovsky, p.51

9   Velikovsky, pp.58-59

10 Prestwich, p.vi

11 Ibid, p.67

12 Ibid, p.7

13 Joseph Prestwich, "The Raised Beaches and 'Head' or Rubble-drift of the South of England," *Quarterly Journal of the Geological Society*, XLVIII, 1892, 319-37; Prestwich, "On the Evidences of a Submergence of Western Europe and of the Mediterranean Coasts at the Close of the Glacial or So-called Post-Glacian Period, and Immediately Preceding the Neolithic or Recent Period," *Philosophical Transactions of the Royal Society of London*, 1893, Series A, 1894, pp. 904ff

14 G. Bush. 1869 "On the caves of Gibraltar in which human remains and works of art have been found." *Int Congr Prehist Archaeol*, Trans, 3rd session, Norwich, 20th-27th August 1868, London 1868, xxx + 419 pp: Bush's paper pp.106-107, p.122

15 Ibid, p.48

16 Rehwinkel, *The Flood*. St Louis, Mo.: Concordia Publishing House, 1951, p.180 (emphasis supplied)

Chapter 6 – THE SUDDENNESS

1   O.P. Hay, *The Pleistocene of the Western Region of North America and its Vertebrate Animals*, Carnegie Institute, Washington, 1927, publ.no. 322B, 346, pp.171-174

2   Price, *The New Geology*, p.579

3   Velikovsky, *Earth in Upheaval*, p.65

4   "Explorations and Field-work of the Smithsonian Institution for the

Year 1913", Washington, 1914, *Annual Report of the Smithsonian Institution for 1918*, pp.281-287

5   Rehwinkel, p.234

6   C.F. Hartt 1870 *Geology and Physical Geography of Brazil*, Boston, xxiii +620 pp; see pp.286-287

7   M. de Nadoillae 1885. *Prehistoric America*, London, xii +566 pp; see p.25

8   Sir Henry Howarth, *The Mammoth and the Flood*, p352ff. London: Sampson, Low, Marston, Searle and Risington, 1998

9   W.A. Clarke 1875. "Remarks on the Sedimentary formations of New South Wales", *Annual Report of the Dept. of Mines*, New South Wales, 3rd ed., pp. 149-206; p.163

10 Dr. Lang 1831. "Account of the discovery of bone caves in Wellington Valley about 210 miles west of Sydney in New Holland", *Edinburgh New Philosophical Journal*, vol. x pp. 364-371; see pp.369-370

11 J.E.T. Woods 1862 *Geological Observations in South Australia, principally in the district SE of Adelaide*, London, xviii +404 pp; see pp.335,385

12 W.B. Clarke, p.164

13 P.S. Pallis, *Travels through the southern provinces of the Russian Emppa in 1793 and 1794*, tr. F.E. Blaydon, vol. 1., p.115, London, 1802

14 Pallis, 1802. see vol.3, p.125

15 (N.A.E. Nordenskiold, *Voyage of the Vega round Asia and Europe*, tr. H. Leslie, London, vol. 1, p.523, 1881)

16 C.F. Rouillier, 1846. "Explication de la coupe geologiques des environs de Moscow", *Bulletin de la Societe des Naturalistes de Moscow*, vol. xix, pt.11, pp. 359-467, p.360

17 R. Moore, *Man, Time and Fossils*, 1953, pp. 274-275

18 Wadia, *Geology of India*, pp. 274-275

19 Velikovsky, *Earth in Upheaval*, p.72

20 Whitcomb and Morris, *The Genesis Flood*. Phillipsburg, N.J.: Presbyterian and Reformed Publishing Co., 1986, p.,161
21 "Adventures in the Search for Man," *National Geographic*, January 1963, p.149
22 L.Dingus and D. Loope. 2000. "Death in the Dunes." *Natural History* 109, no. 6; Orndorff, R. L., et al. 2001. "How the West Was Swum." *Natural History* 110, no. 5; Sereno, P. 1996. "Africa's Dinosaur Castaways." *National Geographic* 189, no. 6
23 Bjorn Kurten, *The Age of Dinosaurs*)
24 *Creation Research News Update No. 5*, April 23, 2003

Chapter 7 – INTERRUPTED DINNER

1 Frank C. Hibben, *The Lost Americans*. New York: Thomas Y. Crowell Company, 1946, p.91
2 Ibid, pp.177,178
3 Gen.8:1
4 *Encyclopaedia Brittanica*, vol.12, 1956. Article "Ivory", p.834
5 Rehwinkel, p.243
6 Charles Berlitz, *Doomsday 1999*. St. Albans, U.K.: Granada, 1982, p.63
7 J.D. Dana, *Manual of Geology*, p.1007
8 George McCready Price, *The New Geology*. Mountain View, California: Pacific Press Publishing Association, 1923, p.654 (emphasis added)
9 Ibid, p.654

10 Harold T. Wilkins, *Mysteries of Ancient South America*. Secaucus, N.J.: Citadel Press, 1974, p.18

11 Whitcomb and Morris, P.290

12 Sir Henry Howorth, *The Mammoth and the Flood*. London: Sampson, Low, Marston, Searle and Risington, 1887, pp.48,49

13 Henry Hiebert, *Evolution: Its Collapse in View*? P.89

14. Ivan Sanderson, "Frozen Mammoths in Siberia" in *The World's Great Unsolved Mysteries*. Ed. Martin Ebon. New York: The New American Library, Inc., 1981, pp.38,39. Important supporting data is found on pp.35-36 and 39-43

15 see page 72

Chapter 8 – THE SECRET OF LOMPOC QUARRY

1 M. Brogersma-Sanders, "Treatise on Marine Ecology and Paleoecology," *Geological Society of America Memoir 67*, 1957, p.972

2 Immanuel Velikovsky, *Earth in Upheaval*. New York: Doubleday and Company, 1955, p.22

3 George McCready Price, *Evolutionary Geology and New Catastrophism*. Mountain View, Calif.: Pacific Press Publishing Association, 1926, p.236

4 Harry S. Ladd, "Ecology, Paleontology, and Stratigraphy," *Science*, vol.129, Jan.9, 1959, p.72

5 Hugh Miller, *The Old Red Sandstone*. Boston: Gould and Lincoln, 1857, p.,221

6 W. Buckland, *Geology and Mineralogy*. Philadelphia, 1837, p.101

7 Ibid, p.103

8 Price, Ibid, pp.235ff (emphasis added)

9 "Workers Find Whale in Diatomaceous Earth Quarry," *Chemical*

and Engineering News, 11 October 1976, p.40

Chapter 9 – SURPRISE FOR ADMIRAL BYRD

1. Harold G. Coffin, *Creation-Accident or Design?* Washington, D.C.: Review and Herald Publishing Association, 1969, p.65
2. E.S. Moore, *Coal: Its Properties, Analysis, Classification, Geology, Extraction, Uses and Distribution.* New York: Wiley, 2nd ed., 1940, p.146
3. Price, *The New Geology.* Mountain View, Calif.: Pacific Press Publishing Association, 1923, p.467
4. Sir Edgeworth David, *Geol. Surv. N.S.W.* Mem. G.4, 1907, p.13
5. vol.262, p.865
6. W.W. Greenman, *Evidences of the Flood.* Harpenden, England: Gospel Standard Strict Baptist Trust, 1977, p.7
7. *Ex Nihilo Technical Journal*, 1985
8. *Bulletin, Geological Society of America*, vol.80, pp.2109-2114
9. *Quarterly Journal, Geological Society of London*, vol.118, p.13
10. R. Hayatsu, *Organic Geochemistry*, Vol. 6, pp.463-471, 1984

Chapter 10 – ONE FLOOD OR MANY?

1. See Book 1 – *The Killing of Paradise Planet*
2. The amount of solar energy falling on the earth's surface in 14 days is equal to the known energy of the world's supply of fossil fuels. Only .03% of the solar energy arriving at the earth's surface is stored as chemical energy in vegetation through photosynthetic processes. Mary Archer, *Journal of Applied Electrochemistry*, vol.5, 1975, p.17. From this data we can estimate how many years of today's plant growth would be required to produce the stored energy in today's known coal reserves. Andrew Snelling has calculated thus:

Divide 14 days by .03%, i.e., 14 x 100,/.03 days equals 46,667 days or 128 years of solar input via photosynthesis

3   "Coal Beds and Noah's Flood", *Creation Ex Nihilo*, June 1986, pp.20,21

4   *Science Digest*, vol.74, p.77

5   *Science*, vol.219, pp.24-26

6   Australian Stock Exchange Release, Environmental Solutions International Limited, Osborne Park, Western Australia, October25, 1996, Media Statement, Minister for Water Resources, Western Australia, October 25, 1996

7   A.I. Levorsen, *Geology of Petroleum*. San Francisco: W.H. Freeman & Co., 1954, p.524

8   P.V. Smith, *Science*, October 24, 1952

9   J.M. Peter, O.E. Kawka, S.D. Scott and B.R.T. Simoneit, 1988. *Third Chemistry Congress of North America, Toronto*, abstract GEOC 036

Chapter 11 – LADY BLUE'S LAST VOYAGE

1   H.T. Wilkins, *Secret Cities of Old South America*, 1952, p.418

2   *The Morrisonville Times*, June 11, 1891; "Mysteries of the Unexplained", N.Y. Reader's Digest, 1982, p.46

3   *The Times*, June 22, 1844

4   *Nature*, Nov.11, 1886, p.36; *L'Astronomie*, Paris, 1887, p.463; J.R. Jochmans, *Strange Relics from the Depths of the Earth*. Lincoln, Nebraska: Forgotten Research Society, 1979, p.2

5   *Saturday Herald*, Iowa City, April 10, 1967

6   M. Rusch, *"Human Footprints in Rocks"*, CRSQ, vol.7, 1970, p.201

7   *American Journal of Science*, 1-144, quoting from *The Minerology of Count Bourbon*

8   *The American Antiquarian*, 1883

9 *Creation Research Society Journal*, 1976
10 *Ex Nihilo*, Vol.1, No.4, International, 1983, p.5
11 *Creation Ex Nihilo*, Nov.1985, pp.14-16
12 Switzerland: B. Fregoso, *De dictis factisqi Memorabilibus Collectanea. Medoliani*, 1509, np), (Russia: P.J. Strahlenberg, *A historico-description of the northern part of North and Eastern Europe and Asia.* London, 1738, 462 pp; see p.405), (South Africa: Anonymous. *General Literature and Miscellaneous Communications:* no 17 "Ship discovered in the Earth in Africa", *1818, QJI Lit Sci Arts Lond, vol. v, p.150*
13 P. Cieza de Leon, *La Cronica del Peru*: Part One. Seville, 1553, pp. xxxii and 367
14 Omaha *Daily News*, 1897
15 Michael A. Crèmo and Richard L. Thompson, *Forbidden Archaeology: The Hidden History of the Human Place.* Badger, CA., 1993; *Nexus*, June-July 1995

Chapter 12 – FOOTPRINTS IN COAL

1 C.M. Chen, Smena, *Russian Journal, No.8, 1961*
2 *Jour Trans Vict. Institute*, 80:21-22
3 Brad Steiger, *Worlds Before Our Own*, pp.48,49
4 Cremo and Thompson, Forbidden Archaeology; *Nexus*, June-July 1995
5 *Mysteries of the Unexplained*, N.Y. Reader's Digest, 1982, p.46. M.Cook, William J. Meister "Discovery of Human Footprint with Trilobites in a Cambrian Formation of Western Utah," *Why Not Creation?* W. Lammerts, ed. N.J.: Presbyterian & Reformed Pub. Co., 1970, pp.185-193
6 M. Leakey and R.L. Hay, *Nature*, March 22, 1979
7 Tulsa *Sunday World*, May 25, 1969

8   *The American Journal of Science*, 3:26, 139-140, July-Dec. 1883

9   R.T. Bird, "Thunder in His Footsteps," *Natural History*, May 1938, p.255

10 J.R. Jochmans, *Strange Relics From the Depth of the Earth*. Lincoln, Nebraska: Forgotten Research Society, 1979, pp.8,9

11 *The American Journal of Science and Arts*, 1:5:223-231, 1822

12 *American Antiquarian*, vol.7, p.39

13 The Field, *Natural History Journal*, 1948

14 Brad Steiger, *Mysteries of Time and Space*. London: Sphere Books Limited, 1974, pp.15-25

15 *Pursuit, Vol.3, No.4*, October, 1970

16 Dr. Wibur Gredy Burroughs, former head of the Geology Department of Berea College, cited by Brad Steiger, *Mysteries of Time and Space*. London: Sphere Books, 1974, p.17

17 *Scientific American*, Jan., 1940 (emphasis supplied)

18 Dr. Burdick *Footprints in the Sands of Time*, cited by Steiger, *Worlds Before Our Own*, pp.48,49

Chapter 13 – MEN IN EMBARRASSING PLACES

1   *The Carbon County News*, Montana, Nov.11, 1926. Ref. 13, M.Y. Reader's Digest, p.46

2   Charles Berlitz, *The Bermuda Triangle*. St. Albans, U.K.: Panther Books, Ltd., 1977, p.179

3   Otto Stutzer, *Geology of Coal*. Trans. By A.C. Noe, Chicago: University of Chicago Press, 1940, p.271. Stutzer was Professor of Geology and Mineralogy in the School of Mines at Freiberg, in Saxony

4   J.R. Jochmans, *Strange Relics From the Depths of the Earth*. Lincoln, Nebraska: Forgotten Research Society, 1979, p.3

5   A. Keith, *The Antiquity of Man*, 1925, pp.335-340. Sergi, Rivista di Anthropologia, vol. XVII. Fasc. I-II, Rome. M. Bowden, Ape-Man: Fact or Fallacy? Bromley, Kent: Sovereign Publication, 1981, pp.79,80

6   B.W.H., "Alleged Discovery of an Ancient Human Skull in California", *American Journal of Science*, 2:42, 1866

7   *Saturday Herald*, Iowa City, April 10, 1867

8   "Ancient Man in Missouri", *Scientific American*, Sept. 1880, p.169

9   Dr. Clifford Wilson, in "Forward" to *The Bible and Science*, by Jeff Harvey and Charles Pallaghy. Blackburn, Victoria, Australia: Acacia Press Pty. Ltd, 1985, p.vi

10 Steiger, *Worlds Before Our Own*, pp.46,47

11 Bob Helfinstine and Bill Overn, *Bible-Science Newsletter*, 2911 East 42nd Street, Minneapolis, MN, August 1987

12 Alexander Romashko, *Moscow News*, 1983; Carl E. Baugh and Clifford A. Wilson, *Dinosaur*. Orange, CA: Promise Publishing, 1991, pp.140-145

13 Erich von Danicken, *According to the Evidence*. London: Souvenir Press, 1977, p.332

14 Peter Kolosimo, *Timeless Earth*. New York: Bantam Books, 1975, p.16

15 Setterfield, *Creation and Catastrophism*, 1993, pp.12-13

16 H.S. Lipson, Professor of Physics, University of Manchester, "A Physicist Looks at Evolution", *Physics Bulletin*, vol.31, 1980 (emphasis added)

17 Michael Walker, Senior Lecturer in Anthropology, Sydney University, *Quadrant*, October, 1981, p.44

Chapter 14 – THE CASE OF THE MISSING BODIES

1   Ralph Buchsbaum, Dept. of Zoology, University of Chicago,

　　　　Animals Without Backbones. Chicago, Ill.: The University of Chicago Press

2　　Ilya Prigogine, Professor and Director of the Physics Department, Universite Libre de Bruxelles, "Can thermo-dynamics explain biological order?" *Impact of Science on Society*, vol.23(3), 1973, p.178. Ernst Chain, world famous biochemist, as quoted by R.W. Clark, in *The Life of Ernst Chain: Penicillan and Beyond.* Weidenfeld & Nicholson, London, 1985, p.148

3　　Professor J. Leconte, Geologist of the University of California. Cited by F.C. Payne, in *The Seal of God*

4　　E.C. Olson, *The Evolution of Life*, 1965, p.94

5　　Darwin, Charles. "On the imperfection of the geological record," Chapter X, *The Origin of Species* London: J.M. Dent & Sons Ltd., 1971, pp.292-293

6　　Darwin's champion, T.H. Huxley. Cited in Graham Rehn's *Creation or Evolution* Adelaide, Australia: Kitchener Press Pty. Ltd., undated, p.17

7　　*Newsweek*, March 29, 1982, p.42

8　　David B. Kitts, Ph.D, Zoology, Head Curator, Department of Geology, Stoval Museum, and well-known evolutionary paleontologist. *Evolution*, vol.28, September 1974, p.467

9　　Ronald R. West, Ph.D, Paleo-ecology and Geology, Assistant Professor of Paleoebiology at Kansas State University, "Paleontology and uniformitarianism." *Compass,* vol. 45, May 1968, p.216

10.　Personal letter, written 10 April 1979, from Dr. Colin Patterson, Senior Paleontologist at the British Museum of Natural History in London, to Luther D. Sunderland; as quoted in *Darwin's Enigma* by Luther D. Sunderland. San Diego, U.S.A.: Master Books, 1984, p.89

11　 Stephen Jay Gould, Professor of Geology and Paleontology, Harvard University, "The return of hopeful monsters", *Natural History, vol. LXXXVI 6*, June-July 1977, p.24

12　 Barbara J. Stahl, St. Anselm's College, U.S.A., *Vertebrate History:*

Problems in Evolution. New York: McGraw-Hill, 1974, pp.349,350

13   Austin H. Clark, *The New Evolution: Zoogenesis.* Baltimore: Williams and Williams Company, 1930, p.181

14   Chester A. Arnold, Professor of Botany and Curator of Fossil Plants, University of Michigan, in *An Introduction to Paleobotany.* New York: McGraw-Hill, 1947, p.7

15   E.J.H. Corner, Professor of Tropical Botany, Cambridge University, U.K., "Evolution" in *Contemporary Botanical Thought*, Anna M. MacLeod and L.S. Cobley, editors, for the Botanical Society of Edinburgh: Oliver and Boyd, 1961, p.97

16   N. Heribert-Nilsson, *Synthetische Artbildung*, Verleg CWH Gleerue 1953, p.1188

17   T. Neville George, "Fossils in Evolutionary Perspective," Science Progress, Jan. 1960, p.3

18   Norman D. Newell, "The Nature of the Fossil Record" *Proceedings of the American Philosophical Society*, April 1959, 103(2), pp.264-285

19   David M. Raup, Curator of Geology, Field Museum of Natural History, Chicago, "Conflicts between Darwin and paleontology", *Field Museum and Natural History Bulletin, vol.50(1),* January 1979, p.25

20   Richard M. Ritland, "Those Missing Links", in *Creation.* Mountain View, Calif.: Pacific Press Publishing Association, p.61

21   *Science*, vol.259, February 5, 1993, p.764. Melbourne *Sun Herald*, February 14, 1993. *Creation Ex Nihilo*, vol.15, No.3, June-August, 1993, p.9

22   Fred John Meldau, *Why We Believe in Creation Not in Evolution*, p.329

23   G.A. Kerkut, *The Implications of Evolution.* New York: Pergamon Press, 1960

24   Norman D. Newell, "The Nature of the Fossil Record," *Proceedings of the American Philosophical Society, April 1959, 103(2),* pp.264-285

25 David B. Kitts, "Paleontology and Evolutionary Theory", *Evolution*, vol.28, Sept.1974, p.467

26 Cited in Graham Rehn's *Creation or Evolution* Adelaide, Australia: Kitchener Press Pty. Ltd., undated, p.17

27 *New York Times*, November 4, 1980

28 D. Dwight Davis, "Comparative Anatomy and the Evolution of Vertebrates", in *Genetics, Paleontology and Evolution*, ed. By Jepsen, Mayr and Simpson. Princeton, N.J.: Princeton University Press, 1949, pp.74,77

29 James W. Valentine and Cathryn A. Campbell, "Genetic Regulation and the Fossil Record", *American Scientist*, vol.63, Nov-Dec 1975, p.673

Chapter 15 – SORRY, NO CHANGE

1 M.E. White, *The Greening of Gondwana*, caption under photograph "Kauri Pine: little change after 175 million years"

2 Austin A. Clark, *The New Evolution: Zoogenesis*. Baltimore: Williams and Williams Company, 1930 (emphasis added)

3 Time-Life book, *Evolution*, 1964, p.42

Chapter 16 – DON'T TRY TO MOVE OLD BEDS

1 Immanuel Velikovsky, *Earth in Upheaval*. London: Sphere Books, Ltd., 1978, p.11

2 F.K. Mather, reviewing G. Gamour, "Biography of the Earth", in *Science*, January 16, 1942

3 Reginald A. Daly, *The Changing World of the Ice Age*, 1934, p.111

4 William Bowie, long-time director of the United States Coast and Geodetic Survey called it "absurd, from an engineering point of

view." M. King Hubbert and William W. Rubey, in an article, "Role of Fluid Pressure in Mechanics of Overthrust Faulting", *Bulletin of Geological Society of America, vol.70*, February 1959, p.126, called it "a mechanical impossibility"

5   Webster's *Third International Dictionary*, unabridged, 1964, p.2498

6   *Evolution: Fact or Belief?* Video produced for Cercle Scientifique Et Historique (CESHE), 9 Ave du General Leclerc 59170 Croix, France

7   Dr. Steve Austin, video, *Mount St Helens: Explosive evidence for catastrophe in Earth's history*

8   P. Stevenson, "Meteorite Evidence for a Young Earth," *Creation Research Society Quarterly 12. June 1975*: 23; cited by R.L. Wysong, *The Creation-Evolution Controversy*. Midland, MI: Inquiry Press, 1976:171

Chapter 17 – WHAT MY TEACHER DIDN'T KNOW

1   Georges Cuvier, *Essay on the Theory of the Earth*, 5th ed., 1827, p.24

2   L.H. Adams, *"Some Unsolved Problems of Geophysics", Transactions, American Geophysical Union, vol.28*. October, 1947, p.676

3   George C. Kennedy, "The Origin of Continents, Mountain Ranges, and Ocean Basins", *American Scientist, vol.47*. December, 1959, p.495

4   Gen.7:21-23 New English Bible

5   Ken Hood, *Warwick Daily News, October 8, 2003*

Chapter 18 – DINOSAUR ALIVE!

1   Adrian Desmond, *The Hot-Blooded Dinosaur: A Revolution in Paleontology.* 1976

2   See our book *The Killing of Paradise Planet*, Chapters 14 and 15

3   *Geological Society of America abstract proceedings*, Vol.17, p.548; Kyle L. Davies, "Duckbill Dinosaurs [Hadrosauridae, Ornithischia] from the North Slope of Alaska", *Journal of Paleontology*, Vol.61 No.1, pp.198-200

4   *New Scientist*, October 31, 1992, p.18

5   Edwin H. Colbert, *The Age of Reptiles*. London: W.W. Norton and Company, Ltd.:1966, p.191

6   *The Weekend Australian*, August 27-28, 1983, p.11. *The Times*, London, August 25, 1983

7   *Time*, June 5, 1985

8   *Gen.6:19-20; 7:15-16*

9   See *The Killing of Paradise Planet*, Chapter 13

10 *Job 40:15-17*

11 A. Hyatt Verill, *Old Civilisations of the New World*. New York: New Home Library, 1943

12 *Prehistoric Indians*, Barnes and Pendleton, 1995, p.201

13 Article by Fred Olsen in *The Daily Colonist*, April 16, 1967

14 Stewart Wavell, *The Lost World of the East*. London: Souvenir Press, 1958

15 Leonard Clark, *The Rivers Ran East*. London: Hutchinson, 1954, p.230

16 *Science Digest*, June, 1981. *Science Frontiers*, no.33

17 Anonymous, "Living Dinosaurs," *Science*-80, vol. 1, November 1980, pp. 6-7

18 Science writer Robert Locke, *Associated Press*, June 11, 1981

19 "Results from the Mokele Mbembe expedition", *Cryptozoology*, 2:103, 1983

20 www.genesispark.org/genpark/mokele/mokele.htm

INDEX

Archaeopteryx 156
Axis tilted 10-15

Boats inside mountains 119

Canopy collapsed 20,21,27
Climate change 25
Coal
- from the Flood 43,91-103
- human relics in 109-142,144,147
Coelancanth 161
Comet hypothesis 13-14,78
Continental split 18
Cracks in earth 18,21,25
Cover-ups 120-121,123,126-127,133-135,143,146-147,174
Creation, fossils consistent with 154, 159,160

Darwin, Charles 143,146,150,152
Dating
- hopelessly in error 144
  (see also: Geology – time scale)
Dinosaurs 43,62-64,85,86,130-140,145,178,194-209
Earthquakes 18-19
Erratic boulders 31-33
Evolution
- proof of, expected from fossils 109-110,152
- no fossil evidence for 150-192 (esp. 159)
- occurring today? 165-166
- not proven 159
- a religion 146-147
- why accepted by scientists 144-147
- rejected by many scientists 147-148
- in schools 143-144

Fire 15-16
Flood:
- one or many? 104-105,190
- not an accident 14
- overtook men and animals 26-27,30,43-44
- events of 10-23,30-31,43-48
- human interest description 9-10,26-27,44,47,109
- acted unevenly in various localities 189
- sources of the water 17,19-21,25-26
- height of the waters 50,54
- depth of sediments 60-61,70,186
- depth of lava flow 24

Footprints: see Tracks
Fossils
- often crushed 61,180
- indicate rapid burial 178,180,189
- in groups 40,43,46
- order of burial 40-42
- fissures of bones 48-66
- frozen graveyards 67-81
- fish, whales 82-90
- land & sea creatures mixed 48-50,52,55,56,59,85,86
- earliest fossils:
  * no ancestors 151
  * already perfect 152
- later fossils:
  * no connecting links 150-160
- earliest forms still living 161-162
- modern descendants unchanged 162-169
- in wrong order 171,174
- all types at bottom 176
- all mixed in same stratum 176-177
- individuals through several strata 95,98,178-179
- fossils still forming now? 184-186
- can form rapidly 188
- no sudden "leaps" 157-158
- do not prove evolution 150-192 (esp. 159)

Gaps in fossils 150-160
Genesis
- reliability of 189-191,210
Genetics 164-166
Geology
- valid without evolution theory 190
- time scale 141,149-150,181,182,188
 (See also: Dating)
Grand Canyon 39,179,182,183

Human remains: see Man

Ice versus water action 32,57,59

Jasher, book of 18

Mammoths 11,49,55,58,59,67-80,190,201
- time taken to freeze 73,78
Man, in all strata "ages" 109-142
Mars 13
Microwave effect 28-29
Moon 13
Mountains covered by the Flood 23,34-35,48-52,54

Oil 19,107-108
Overthrusting 172-175

Petrified forests 105
Pillow lava 23
Planets 13
Polystrate fossils 95,98,99,178-179
Preservation of remains 49,50,56,62,68-69,73,83-84
Punctuated equilibrium 157-158

Rain of the Global Flood, source of 25-26
Rapid burial, see Sudden event

Scientists
- why many accept evolution 144-147
- many now reject evolution 147-148

Sudden event, not gradual (incl. rapid burial) 11,61,62,64,69,73,75-78,83-86,89,94,96,102,178,180,189

St. Helens, Mount 22,99,106-107,178,188

Strata:
- in wrong order 171,174
- all "types" at bottom 176-177
- no time lapse between 179-181
- not formed by gradual submergence and raising 183
- thickness of sediment 60-61,70,186
- how it was formed 183-192
- builds sideways 172
- "missing" strata 175
- bent while soft 180

Suddenness of the Great Flood 11,55-64

Thermonuclear meltdown 17,20,27-29
Tidal waves and tsunamis 21,23,30-35,45-46
Tracks 39-40,122-127,130-133
Trilobites 124,125,127,137-139
Tsunamis 21,30-32,33
Tuatara 161-162

Underground basins 19,21,27-28
Uniformitarianism not an adequate explanation 186

Variation within species 164-166
Volcanism 21-28
- caused great rain 25-26

Venus 13

Water, sources of 17,19-21,25-26
Waves, power of 31-35
Whales 49,86-88

Yellowstone 105-106

"The Invitation" – A fine art print by Elfred Lee

THOUSANDS OF YEARS AGO OUR ANCESTORS MADE ONE LAST DECISION...

WHO WOULD ACCEPT THE INVITATION?

"ON AN EXPEDITION IN 1969, ON A TREELESS MOUNTAIN THE BIBLE NAMES AS THE RESTING PLACE OF NOAH'S ARK, WE UNEARTHED 5,000-YEAR-OLD WOOD, MAKING ME REALIZE THE STORY WAS TRUE. THIS ALMOST MYSTICAL EXPERIENCE COMPELLED ME TO PAINT 'THE INVITATION'."
– ELFRED LEE

SAVE UP TO $320
USE PROMO CODE
BSW003
LITHOGRAPHS
STARTING AT $99
WWW.LOSTWORLDMUSEUM.COM

FINE ART PRINT

CANVAS LITHO

Limited edition – Order yours today.
LOST WORLD MUSEUM

WWW.LOSTWORLDMUSEUM.COM
ORDER TOLL FREE: 1-866-593-3010

We invite you to view the complete
selection of titles we publish at:

www.TEACHServices.com

or write or email us your praises,
reactions, or thoughts about this
or any other book we publish at:

TEACH Services, Inc.
P.O. Box 954
Ringgold, GA 30736

info@TEACHServices.com

Finally, if you are interested in seeing
your own book in print, please contact us at

publishing@teachservices.com.

We would be happy to review your manuscript for free.

www.ingramcontent.com/pod-product-compliance
Lightning Source LLC
Chambersburg PA
CBHW070549160426
43199CB00014B/2429